Start Your Own

ONLINE EDUCATION BUSINESS

Additional titles in *Entrepreneur's* ***Startup Series***

Start Your Own

Bar or Club

Bed & Breakfast

Business on eBay

Business Support Service

Car Wash

Child Care Service

Cleaning Service

Clothing Store

Coin-Operated Laundry

Consulting

Crafts Business

e-Business

e-Learning Business

Event Planning Business

Executive Recruiting Service

Freight Brokerage Business

Gift Basket Service

Growing and Selling Herbs and Herbal Products

Home Inspection Service

Import/Export Business

Information Consultant Business

Law Practice

Lawn Care or Landscaping Business

Mail Order Business

Medical Claims Billing Service

Personal Concierge Service

Personal Training Business

Pet-Sitting Business

Restaurant and Five Other Food Businesses

Retail Business and More

Seminar Production Business

Staffing Service

Travel Business

Vending Business

Wedding Consultant Business

Wholesale Distribution Business

Entrepreneur MAGAZINE'S

startup

Start Your Own

ONLINE EDUCATION BUSINESS

Your Step-by-Step Guide to Success

Entrepreneur Press and Rich Mintzer

EP
Entrepreneur Press

Editorial Director: Jere L. Calmes
Managing Editor: Marla Markman
Cover Design: Beth Hansen-Winter
Production and Composition: Eliot House Productions

Library of Congress Cataloging-in-Publication Data

Mintzer, Richard.
Start your own online education business/by Entrepreneur Press and Rich Mintzer.
p. cm.
ISBN-13: 978-1-59918-120-2 (alk. paper)
ISBN-10: 1-59918-120-7 (alk. paper)
1. Computer-assisted instruction. 2. Education—Data processing. 3. New business enterprises. 4. Entrepreneurship. I. Entrepreneur Press. II. Title.

LB1028.5.M557 2007
371.33'40681—dc22 2007023250

Printed in Canada
12 11 10 09 08 07 10 9 8 7 6 5 4 3 2 1

Contents

Preface

We're living in the incredible Information Age. In no other time in history has the acquisition and appropriate application of knowledge been so important or so challenging. The personal computer and the internet not only make vast stores of information available, they also make that information essential to our personal and financial well-being.

No longer is the computer the domain of a geeky priesthood of geniuses in white frock coats laboring long hours over arcane and complex programs. The personal computer has become nearly as pervasive as the telephone or television.

Children are introduced to computers in elementary school. They soon master e-mail, report writing, internet access, and dozens of other common applications that not long ago were the exclusive province of technicians with million-dollar equipment.

The real value of a computer isn't that it can do a better job than an array of old tools such as typewriters and fax machines. Rather, the computer has become the key that unlocks vast stores of constantly changing information. The ability to navigate the internet has become a professional necessity for most white-collar and many blue-collar jobs.

On the lighter side, the computer also provides personal enrichment and recreation. There are no limits to its functionality, to the imagination of the people using it, or to your opportunities in opening up that functionality to help people learn.

Today, online education covers a broad spectrum. From teaching grade-schoolers, to undergraduate and graduate-level college classes, to adult ed electives, you'll find a wide range of educational options.

Education in this society never ends. Keeping up with the latest information is vital. What you learned five years ago, three years ago, or even a year ago may already be obsolete, especially in the area of technology. So the days of putting away the schoolbooks after obtaining your technical college or post-graduate degree are long gone. Education must now be an ongoing process. In fact, many fields, including teaching, real estate, and medicine require continuing course work.

Getting Started as an Online Learning Entrepreneur

You no longer need an educational background to be involved in the education industry. The field is relatively open for anyone from any background who wants to provide instruction in almost anything—and to those who develop the infrastructure, content, and other supporting services necessary for delivering instruction. An educational background can help, but it does not seem to be a prerequisite for most start-up online learning businesses. The best candidates to start such a business are the same individuals best suited for other ventures—plain old entrepreneurs with lots of imagination and persistence.

Your place in the online learning industry is limited only by your imagination. It's an industry that barely existed a decade ago, and it will continue to grow and change in ways that can't be foreseen. Entrepreneurs have already come up with some truly ingenious entrées, and in this start-up guide we'll explore some of the ways successful entrepreneurs did it. But there are no cookie-cutter approaches. Many such businesses prosper. Others fail.

This book features interviews with industry experts and educators, market analysts, and the founders of online education ventures, both large and small. We'll look at how successful online learning entrepreneurs define their missions, how they raise money, how they approach marketing, and how they handle the 10,000 other tasks that the chief cook and bottle washer faces every day.

Throughout the book you'll find tip boxes with information on the industry as well as helpful ideas and advice for running an online education business. An appendix filled with resources is at the back of the book.

Good luck in your quest to be an online education entrepreneurial success.

1

Learning for a Better Life

Knowledge is the coin of this realm. Unless you're a movie star, professional athlete, or perhaps the inventor of some amazing new product, what you know is far more important than just about anything else in the business game. To hold your own in the marketplace, you've got to keep learning—everything from changing social norms to the latest management theories to mastery of technologies that didn't even exist a few years ago. That's true in boon times and in bad times.

From business learning to courses that keep the mind sharp and active, there are a wide range of markets for online education. In this chapter, we'll look at the circumstances that make education so important and how these circumstances open up opportunities for you, the entrepreneur.

A Degree of Confidence

At the beginning of the 20th century, if you had just some high school education, you could get a fairly good job. After World War II, a high school education became a necessity. Through the 1960s, if you had a little college—not necessarily even a full degree, but some post-secondary training—you enjoyed an edge that would get you a white-collar job. Now, a college degree is just the ante you must have to gain meaningful employment—and ongoing education is a must for many professions.

Job applicants today find it advantageous to show that they have some specific experience in the job for which they are applying. An increasing number of students supplement their college degrees with post-graduate work, technical certifications, and specialty training such as management seminars. Today, ongoing education and letters after your name can make a great deal of difference in competitive fields. And getting degrees, certificates, and ongoing education is no longer strictly for the younger set. It's a prerequisite for professionals of all ages looking to continue climbing the ladder. In most industries, there are degrees and certificates available that show expertise in specific areas within the broader profession. It is this ongoing need for education that has been the impetus for the steadily growing online education industry, fueled largely by the increased pace of technology.

The online education entrepreneur has many options today. Companies need to make sure employees at all levels are up to speed on job requirements. That may mandate technical training, guidance on meeting regulatory standards, or management courses on issues such as sexual harassment and/or hiring/firing.

Ongoing education can be as ambitious as getting your MBA, or it can be very fine-grained.

> Tip...
>
> **Smart Tip**
>
> U.S. corporations planned to spend over $2 billion in 2007 on web-based learning, according to market researcher Adventures. Catering to corporations represents a home-run opportunity for an online education entrepreneur, simply because of the size of each deal. Selling a course to a corporation can touch thousands of employees and lead to follow-up sales. The sale, however, will not be quick.

“A lot of the online training is just getting people familiar with Microsoft Word®,” says John Dalton, analyst with Forrester Research, a technology analysis firm. “It’s not high-level stuff.”

Training can be refreshers on basic material, since “the basics” often change every year. For instance, software tools are constantly being upgraded, with new versions of familiar products as well as new tools for building advanced web pages. There are numerous options. You can resell products. You can broker classes on behalf of other businesses, resell CD-based courses, or engage in other middleman activities in the e-learning economy.

Ongoing training, however, is in no way limited to computers or even technology. While online education is delivered over the internet, it need not be about the internet, or computers at all for that matter. Online education can provide college-level accredited courses for someone who left a traditional college early and never got his or her degree. It can take the form of additional resources and homework help for young students in the K–12 years. It can provide courses for nine to fivers looking to fulfill personal interests or to pursue a second career. It can also be learning option for seniors who want to keep their minds busy and active, or start a business venture.

Degrees can certainly help in various aspects of a career, but knowledge alone is still a winning proposition in a culture that has frequently lost sight of the importance of education in recent years.

Education Pays

Here are the median incomes of full-time workers aged 25 and older by educational attainment. Median individual income based on U.S. Census figures:

Doctorate	$73,892
Professional degree	$71,240
Master’s degree	$58,708
Bachelor’s degree	$48,724
Associate degree	$36,348
Some college, no degree	$33,950
High school diploma	$30,316
Some high school, no diploma	$21,268

Learning Goes Online

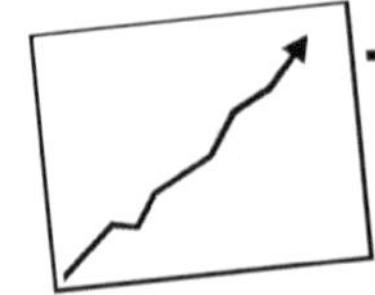

Stat Fact

The median time on the job for the average worker is 3.5 years, according to the Bureau of Labor Statistics. Therefore, a typical 22-year-old college grad will change jobs eight times before age 32.

The seminal event for online education was the internet, which became a vital part of our culture almost overnight. Computer equipment had been applied to education for decades, but when everyone hooked their computers up to the same communication backbone, online learning really kicked into high gear.

In a cover story, *Business Week* identified education as one of five sectors that would be revolutionized by the internet. There are more for-profit education ventures than ever before, but we've barely gotten off the ground. Distance learning has not even been fully explored and exploited, but it has changed the way education is created and presented. Students can now learn at a time and place of their own choosing, and at their own pace. They can utilize data and resources from numerous sources. Students can also enter virtual classrooms led by instructors in other parts of the country, or even the world, and take part in real-time courses from the comfort of their own homes.

Regular (traditional) classroom settings, of course, are not going away. However, the opportunity to learn online has opened up the door to many students who were stymied by time and travel constraints. The full-time work force can now get degrees and certifications or simply take classes for personal enrichment that they would never have had the time or opportunity for pre-internet.

In some cases, the best of both worlds can flourish. Often the most effective online education happens when combined with classroom teaching—often called blended learning. Online educational learning ventures have discovered that one-on-one contact with instructors is an important element of some courses or preferred by some students. For example, the 50,000-plus students at University of Phoenix Online can complete their entire graduate degrees online, including all administration, registration, and book buying if they wish. But the university also has developed a learning option in which students can meet for the first and last class of each course and complete the rest of their classes over the internet, thus providing them with the classroom dynamic as well as the benefits of online learning. Blended learning is discussed in Chapter 6.

What's Your Role?

Online education is a multibillion-dollar market. And, there really are no limits to the subjects that can be delivered via the internet. People have a growing appetite for topics and interests that once seemed far beyond their reach, and companies have an insatiable need to keep employees up-to-speed.

You can pick among many roles in the online learning environment. You can specialize in teaching both large or small businesses, computer basics, management techniques, or high-end programming skills. You might create guides that help employees understand their firm's idiosyncratic software, or interactive content that explains complicated products to customers.

There are endless variations in audience demographics, delivery methods, content, and learning styles. Online learning is wide open. Your ability to mine these opportunities depends on how well your skill set and delivery abilities match with these opportunities.

In the chapters that follow, we discuss how you prepare an online learning business, which entails technical, academic, marketing, and financial know-how. Of course, you need not have all of these skills. You can, instead, build a team around you to handle these aspects of the online education business.

Prior to starting any business venture, you will want to learn about the industry. Knowing what is happening in the online education market, as well as the key words and the various options open to you is discussed in Chapter 2.

Stat Fact

As many as 92 percent of employees say the ability to work from home is an important factor when deciding whether to accept a new job, according to the career web site True Careers (www.truecareers.com). It seems only logical, then, that many people want to learn from the comfort of their own homes.

2

Entering the Online Learning Market

In this chapter, we'll give you an overview of the market, discuss how some online education entrepreneurs have approached the industry, and tackle the fundamentals of how you can go about finding your unique place.

The Education Industry

In many respects, the pursuit of knowledge—including pre- and post-secondary schooling, job training, technical training, and continuing education of all stripes—hasn't changed in decades. Online learning is simply a new, high-tech means of communicating knowledge, just as word processors and spreadsheets were new ways of satisfying the financial needs of businesses at the start of the PC era. The great news for you, the online education entrepreneur, is that this market is not a flash in the pan or a passing fad.

Online education breaks into four main markets, with considerable overlap among them.

1. *Educating children and young adults*. This is one of the largest industries. Some $100 billion a year is spent on this market, and the amounts continue to rise. If you add up all of the online educational products, systems, and services, and include that share of technological infrastructure and administration that these educational institutions can attribute to electronic education, you have around $5 billion in revenues today.
2. *The corporate and business market*. This massive market involves the training of both workers and computer-savvy IT (information technology) professionals. This also includes the many certificate and professional growth courses that credential both employers and employees currently in the work force. Researchers see these markets continuing to grow as competition and the need to keep up with technical growth continue to be essential.
3. *The graduate degree*. Online MBA students are a very large segment of the internet learning base. Courses from strictly online learning ventures as well as traditional universities with online learning programs are included here. These students could be considered part of the business market, but they also overlap with the adult learning market because graduate programs are not limited to business and technical degrees.
4. *Adult learning, or the quest for continuing education*. This is the hardest area to

Stat Fact

According to research by the Sloan Consortium, online education has been growing steadily each year. In the fall of 2002, nearly 1.6 million students were enrolled in at least one online course. In the fall of 2003, the number was close to 2 million, and in 2004, it neared 2.4 million. By the fall of 2005, it topped the 3 million mark and by the fall of 2006, there were more than 3.4 million students taking at least one online course.

quantify because courses and seminars are taken for personal enrichment and/or enjoyment. It's a market that will continue to grow as retirees, stay-at-home moms and/or dads, and even young adults find new subjects to explore. An internet course on genealogy, an interactive guide to understanding the latest electronic gizmo, or an instructor-led virtual tour of the world's great art museums are all possibilities for anyone with a computer, internet hookup, and the desire (and time) to learn something new.

Beware of Geeks Bearing Gifts

Multibillion dollar markets with a zillion niches get people excited, sometimes overly excited. Buzz words like "revolutionize" and "paradigm shift" are tossed around. Before you buy into them, remember the history of the Macarena and Razor scooters.

Why the discouraging words? For one thing, because there is always a lot of hype surrounding any new movement, particularly one heavily based on technology.

As an online education entrepreneur, you must ignore the hype. You must spend serious time learning the rules by which educators in your corner of the market play as opposed to simply assuming that your technology will rewrite the rules. On a practical level, you must accurately comprehend the true nature of the particular opportunity on which you embark. That's tough because markets are always changing. You don't always get reliable news of macro- or micro-economic shifts until it's too late.

But education isn't a market that must be created; it must only be converted to online learning. You have the advantages of a proven, ongoing need. You are swimming downstream in just one tributary of a very large river.

Where Do You Fit In?

What do you want to do with the rest of your life? You need to make money, but after that, how do you want to spend your day? You must brainstorm about how to match your interests, skills, and temperament with the right market opportunities. To get the juices flowing, here are some common entrepreneurial "job" descriptions in online education. As always in this industry, some may overlap.

- *Instructor-led online learning provider*. Students can access your education or training over the internet whenever they want ("asynchronously"), or you can deliver real-time virtual classes through various communications technologies ("synchronously"). A background in education is a plus here because you want

which are we?

Your Online Learning Vocabulary

Before embarking on any entrepreneurial path, it's important that you understand the key terms that you'll be hearing and reading about as you enter the field. Here are a few of the online learning terms you should know (see these and more in the Glossary).

- *Accreditation.* Having approval to give educational credits because your knowledge base formally meets the standards and requirements of a university, government, trade, or other recognized accrediting agency.
- *Asynchronous learning.* Learning through the use of asynchronous communication, that is, with a delay in the interaction. Self-paced courses, courses on CD-Rom, as well as those via e-mail or even on message boards all fall into this category because there is a time gap until the respondent communicates a message back. Students can, therefore, maintain their own pace.
- *Chat.* A situation whereby two or more people are typing messages in an online room or forum. Chats are often used for discussions of course work with other students or with the instructor, in a synchronous real-time learning environment.
- *Computer based training (CBT).* A fully automated learning environment whereby there is no actual instructor. All of the work is preprogrammed and designed so that the student interacts with the computer for assignments, tests or quizzes, questions and answers, etc. This system requires advanced technical training to set up and maintain.
- *Concentration.* A specific area of study, such as business or marketing, in which the student takes a set of courses, typically for a degree in a particular area.
- *Distance education.* From the old correspondence courses (by snail mail) to the modern online educational courses that you will be offering, learning in which the two parties (student and instructor) are not in the same location is considered distance learning. Face-to-face learning (F2F), with student and educator in the same place, is the opposite.
- *Syllabus.* The overview of the course as set out by the instructor, typically within the parameters of the school and/or state requirements. The syllabus includes the course goals and objectives as well as the books that will be used, reports and other assignments, tests to be given, and so on.
- *Synchronous learning.* Learning takes place with both parties participating at the same time without delay in the communication.

Your Online Learning Vocabulary, continued

- *Threaded discussion.* Messages posted on the same topic, often used in online education. The common theme threads the messages together. This is one means by which students can interact with each other as well as with the instructor.
- *Virtual classroom.* An online classroom in cyberspace that doesn't actually exist in the real world. This is the typical online learning environment.

to make your student consumers feel that they are being served well. Your start-up costs are not small—you must hire instructors (at least on a contract basis). You also must create or license a sophisticated delivery mechanism that gets content to your students over the internet. Fortunately, you also may be able to create "canned" content based on your course selection. The bottom line is that you are offering original content and presenting it as an online school or e-learning center.

- *Content provider.* You're the creator here. You specialize in developing the actual educational material; others may package and deliver it. You may use standard software programs or create your own specialized tools for this. Start-up costs can be relatively low, depending on the talent and technologies employed. (Video, for instance, can get expensive very quickly.) This area also requires a background in education or a thorough knowledge of specific content areas. It also requires that you, or someone working with you, knows how to produce educational content in a form that can be marketed and sold.
- *Exam preparation site.* You provide a web site where students can prepare for exams. The site could be oriented toward almost anything from the SATs to preparing for the written test for a driver's license. You post dummy tests with sample questions that show what students can expect from the real exam. You also may provide interactive forums where students discuss issues, with a wealth of related content. Your revenue model is primarily subscriptions with additional potential for advertisements and site referrals. These sites are particularly popular among IT workers preparing for certifications.

Tip...

Smart Tip

One of the most in-demand entrepreneurs today will be the educational consultant who goes into a corporate environment to determine individual training needs and creates a curriculum that is specifically geared toward that company.

- *Certification provider*. You provide course training plus a test that leads to certification in a professional area. Your biggest struggle will be in marketing; you must establish a brand or be validated by a large partner or specific company, such as Microsoft or Oracle.
- *Web aggregator*. Here, you are essentially building a web portal offering a one-stop shop for students to look at online learning opportunities as featured by various universities and/or other established learning environments. This demands that you establish partnership deals with institutions offering online education. The infrastructure is time consuming and costly at the beginning. Once you are established, however, it is less costly to maintain than producing original courses.
- *Reseller and middleman*. This is a catch-all category of activities that can serve any or all of the online education audiences. Some firms resell courses. Others provide consulting services for companies looking to build their training programs. Still others customize content for various educational web sites or serve the technical needs of the online education industry by videotaping courses or setting up an infrastructure. You also might provide news, analysis, or market research about the industry.

Bright Idea

Reaching people who want to get into information technology fields can be tough because they are so spread out geographically. You may be able to attract them through advertising in local periodicals serving college campuses.

Don't be hamstrung by these categories; they are not absolute. While all are challenging, none of these roles need be restrictive, and no one says you can't grow your organization to fill more than one niche. Find a need and fill it!

The four basic principles to consider for online education to be effective are:

1. *Curriculum*. What knowledge will you be imparting?
2. *Students*. Who will be learning and what motivates them to do so?
3. *Marketing*. How will people know about your business?
4. *Technology*. How will you travel through cyberspace?

These are the areas to think about before hiring instructors or IT experts, or setting your course fees. Establishing a foundation on which you will build is the key to planning effectively and efficiently as an entrepreneur.

Curriculum Concerns

This is where you as a painter would have a blank canvas on which to paint that first broad stroke. Is it bright yellow, dark gray, or a mix of a couple of your favorite colors? Likewise, it is a broad stroke that will determine whether you will be teaching basic addition and subtraction to second graders, accredited English literature, and integrated algebra to college students, the latest in wireless technologies to IT professionals, new marketing and account management systems to corporate execs, or introductory French or Italian to retirees who are planning to travel abroad.

Thanks to educators, researchers, historians, librarians, writers, archivists, archeologists, scientists, data processors, and numerous others who have gathered information and recorded it, we have a boundless landscape of educational possibilities from which to choose. Furthermore, almost everyone is a potential student because in our culture it is never too late to learn something new.

Whether you choose to impart your own knowledge and expertise or hire professionally trained people to teach for your business, you will want to have a business to which you feel connected. This isn't to say that you can't simply run the company from afar and be successful, but it is usually beneficial to have some connection. Several online, as well as traditional, learning centers offering a variety of courses have failed because the message from the top was "teach anything that people might want to learn" rather than, "we teach x, y, and z, and we teach them very well."

Of course, part of your decision process will be dictated by the basics of starting any new business. Funding, time commitment, expertise, and human resources always factor into the equation when formulating, and subsequently starting, a new business. The same holds true for online education. It's very hard to start a fully accredited online college if you are working alone, with limited funds, and holding

On-the-Job Training

One possibility, among many, is to offer on-the-job training. It's almost always cheaper to provide incremental training to an existing employee than to train a new one from scratch. Companies struggle to find ways to keep good employees and those in hard-to-find skill categories; that's true even in a recession. Employers have a strong incentive to keep moving lower-level employees up the skills ladder, offering in-house training programs. This represents an obvious opportunity for an entrepreneur.

"The more open-minded organizations are increasingly looking toward their internal workforce, and redeveloping those individuals," reports Kevin Rosenberg, principal of BridgeGate, a recruiting organization in Irvine, California. Rosenberg forecasts a growth in companies "reinvesting in people so they learn new skills, tools, techniques, and technologies."

down a part-time job to maintain a steady source of income. However, starting an online after-school tutoring business might fit the bill. Base the size and scope of your online education endeavor on how much funding, time, and expertise you have, as well as who you have to help you. Typically the technical infrastructure, the curriculum, and the financial/administrative duties are divided up among a team of at least three people when trying to launch even a relatively small online education venture. Still, there are some who have tackled the whole enchilada themselves.

What Do Your Students Want?

Your target student population is huge. No longer does education revolve around the 18- to 22-year-old college student. Instead, the range is from 9 to 90. But what is it that motivates people to take courses on the internet?

Some of the typical motivational factors that lead prospective students to your web site are:

- Maintaining job skills
- Advancing skills, with certifications or degrees
- Learning basics of computers and/or other technology
- Learning advanced technologies and procedures
- Getting a college or graduate degree
- Continuing college or post-grad education
- Learning about an interest or hobby

Why Students Go Online

Students report they use the internet most often to:

Communicate socially	42%
Engage in work for classes	38%
Be entertained	10%
Communicate professionally	7%
Not sure	2%

Source: Pew Internet & American Life Project College Students Survey.

- Getting out of a traffic ticket by going to online traffic school (really!) or solving some similar personal need.

It is important that you focus on one or several of these motivating factors as you plan and prepare for an online education business. It is also important that you determine the characteristics and demographics of your target market.

Market Research

Throughout the book we discuss marketing, or the means by which you will promote and sell your product—online education. Your initial marketing plan will factor into your ability to raise the necessary capital to get the business off the ground. A forerunner of your marketing plan will be doing market research. It is this research that helps you zero in on, and determine how to reach, your prospective students.

Market research is many things to many people. To outfits like Procter & Gamble or Coca-Cola, it means spending tens of millions of dollars on empirical surveys and consumer focus groups to find out if people respond to "lemony fresh" or need a tad more zing in their flavored sugar water. To others, it means looking for a product or service that they themselves want and finding that no one seems to offer it.

Market research may be as simple as taking an informal poll of friends, family, and acquaintances, asking them about their continuing education needs. It may be as complicated and expensive as hiring a professional market research firm to do the legwork and prepare a report. It might mean asking questions in education-related chat rooms, blogs, or online bulletin boards.

Nothing beats getting to know your audience and communicating with the people directly. That's how the co-founders of Spry Learning discovered they needed to redefine their product plans—by volunteering their time at senior centers prior to launching the company. In corporations, you might pick the brains of executives, managers, or other employees who are willing to talk with you. In schools, you might ask a teacher to let you sit in on his or her classes or question students about what would help their studies. You might show them coursework you've developed to get some constructive criticism. You might even do some tutoring, to help get that reality check. Talking with college students about how they plan to pursue their post-graduate level courses might be an effective way to determine how many have considered online learning and how many would consider it if approached by someone like you with a program that meets their post-graduate needs.

Don't forget the internet. Both Spry Learning and MySoftWareHelper swear by the Net for market research. Whatever it is you're looking for, however parochial your need may seem to you, it's probably covered on the Net. "You can find anything online," says Devin Williams, co-founder of Spry.

While this is true to an extent, it does not answer all of your specific needs because your business has not yet begun and factors, such as your specific experience, finances, and technology are not always identical to that which you read about on the internet. Any business that asks humans to do something (such as spend money) needs to factor in human emotions and responses. Use the internet, but also remember that nothing can truly replace the person-to-person response, whether on the telephone, in person, or even through e-mail.

Search and Research

It's up to you to figure out the right market approach, and then do it the right way to get the right picture. Try to gain an understanding of what your potential customers need in the broadest sense. Yes, the conclusion of your research might be that there is a crying need for asynchronous courses to help people qualify for the Microsoft Certified Systems Engineers (MCSE) test. But who knows how long that opportunity will last? Then what—what is the deeper need, the broader market?

Assuming you'd like to stay in business for more than a year or two, what will you do for an encore? What if your vision and/or skills cannot take you to the wider opportunities and enable you to keep pace as a hot market opportunity migrates to other software platforms? Your market advantage must be something deeper than just being another provider of generic courses or certifications—even if it's just having good business sense. In many ways, that's the best market advantage of all.

Utilizing Your Research

One of the pitfalls for many businesses is that after they do their market research they do not properly analyze the responses. In some cases, they even ignore the very research that they spent time and/or money to obtain.

Utilizing market research means creating a profile of your typical customers and determining what it is that they want that you can provide. It is then seeing how much it would cost to "give the people what they want" and finally whether you could sustain a business doing so. Could you set up an infrastructure to provide the type of courses that your research says are in demand? Could you hire experts in the field to teach such courses? Perhaps you can use Computer Based Training (CBT). You need to use your market research as a guide and plan your marketing based on what you have learned from both primary and secondary resources.

One of the key factors that will come out of research is how much a student will spend on a given course or an educational CD-ROM. Pricing is often driven in part by your market research. Therefore, take your time when doing market research and continue to hone your questions and evaluate responses as you go. You should

What Customers Pay to Play

Here are some samples among the wildly varying prices for online learning products and services.

K–12 tutorial session	$25–$100/hour
Interactive CD-ROM for K-12 courses	$15–$60
Asynchronous online general interest course	$50–$200 per course
Instructor-led noncredit college course online	$50–$200 per course
Instructor-led college credit course	$500 and way up per course
High-volume corporate course on general business topics	$20 per student and way up
Interactive CD-ROM on business productivity or IT training	$40–$500
Multi-user network license for business productivity or IT training	$4,500–$10,000 per license
Interactive asynchronous course developed especially for a corporation	$5,000 and way, way up
Instructor-led course custom-developed for a corporation	$20,000 and up

learn from your market research and not be married to any one idea. In fact, after you do your research, you may have to change your plan. Here's one striking example: The co-founders of Spry Learning (www.sprylearning.com) in Portland, Oregon, thought they'd be selling communication equipment to separated family members. But after doing some market research, they wound up developing courseware and instructing trainers how to teach basic computer skills to seniors living in retirement communities.

Don't forget to find out who is competing against you. That shouldn't be too tough because they should be visible any place you could sell your products or services. Make a list and start building a profile of each. Sample their products or services if possible. Then figure out what they're not offering. There will always be people willing to pay more for something better. You just have to figure out what competitive edge you can establish and then find those people willing to pay more for that "special something" that you offer.

Market Research Checklist

Market research need not be costly or time-consuming, and you can more than likely do it yourself. Here's a checklist to make sure you cover the basics.

- ❑ Loosely identify the type of individuals you want to target (seniors, career people, children, other online education companies, or several groups).
- ❑ Conduct your demographic and business research to determine if there are sufficient members of your target audience within your reach.
- ❑ Find out who else is targeting this audience, and make a list of your competition.
- ❑ Look at your competitors' brochures, advertisements, and web sites. Determine what they're offering beyond the basics and what they're charging. List their pros and cons.
- ✓ Find an opening, a niche, a weakness, or some other way to differentiate your business and provide you with your competitive edge.
- ❑ Put a brief description of your offering before some representatives of your target audience to see if they would be interested. Skip the sales pitch—just gather information about what kinds of learning they're interested in and how much they would pay. Take your time when compiling any research questions, surveys, questionnaires, etc. Make sure you are asking questions that provide you with quality responses.
- ❑ Spend some personal time as close to your audience as possible.
- ❑ Adjust your initial impressions and redefine your market approach when necessary. In other words, change the questions to become more specific as you get to know your target market.
- ❑ Compile your data, store it, analyze it, and utilize your market research efforts to help you draw up a plan for your business.

Technology: Tools for School

The fourth element of online education, along with what you're teaching, to whom you are teaching, and how you are marketing your product, is technology. It is technology that puts your courses or your school in cyberspace, making it accessible to your students. It is also technology that can help you serve as the middleperson with a business that helps consumers decide between courses at a variety of learning institutions.

Basic computer skills today begin at a very young age. America's public school systems have bought into personal computers big time. There's now about one computer per four children, and increasingly those computers are reasonably powerful and connected to the internet. Some schools today are equipped with a computer infrastructure that would put many businesses to shame. And of course, the vast majority of schoolchildren today have either their own computer or access to a family computer.

Bright Idea

Recruiters, especially those who specialize in high-tech jobs, can be a good source of customers. Consider giving them a commission for referring students.

Schoolchildren routinely do research on the Net, and their classes often have electronic pen pals in another state or continent. High school students may take virtual courses with other students spread across the country.

For an entrepreneur, there are a variety of approaches to take to the educational market for children and teens. For example, while the home-schooling market remains small, it is perhaps more open to online education, especially if it supports a particular cultural or religious approach to learning. Another hot area is in preparing students for nationwide standardized tests, which have increased in recent years as a result of the No Child Left Behind initiative. While most educators agree that the initiative has been a bust, it still leaves behind a vast amount of testing. Although it handcuffs teachers by having them constantly preparing students for tests, it has been a boost for online test preparation web sites.

On the college scene, online education has made great strides. It's getting harder to find a college or university that doesn't offer at least some online opportunities. At many institutions, incoming students must buy a computer and increasingly campuses are networked not only with conventional wires but also with wireless networks. Instructor-led courses range from very simple asynchronous presentations of text and graphics (with a discussion forum) to computer-enhanced classes that are broadcast in video simultaneously to students in the United States and Singapore. The student population includes not only the 18–22 year olds but also an increasing number of older students returning to complete college degrees. Opportunities abound here—if you can find the right niche and fulfill its requirements.

Keep on Keeping Online

Not long ago, if you wanted to learn something after graduation, you either picked up a book and taught yourself or you enrolled in a continuing education class at a training center or community college. If you took the class, you drove there two or

Tackling Tech Support

When you offer a web course, who do your students call if they experience technical difficulties? If it's a question an instructor can answer by e-mail or maybe even the phone in just a couple of minutes, you may want to offer this as a value-added service at no extra charge. After all, most students will probably have friends in the same boat, and if you go that extra mile for them, they'll recommend your courses.

Computer technology is the tool that keeps your business afloat. Don't make it a stumbling block that gets between you and your students or you and your instructors. As soon as people encounter technical problems that are not easy to solve or require them to pay additional money, they will find an online education provider with more user-friendly tech support. This is one area not to over look. Be as consumer tech friendly as possible.

three times a week, sat in a classroom, and soaked up knowledge as best you could. Time and space were probably more of a worry than tuition. As you got further along on the work treadmill, it became tougher and tougher to find the time to continue your education.

The internet is what conquers time and space for online learning. Entrepreneurial pioneers have been offering computer-based training for decades. But the internet was their definitive "ah-ha!" moment. "We have this new paradigm of so-called lifelong learning that is being driven by the fact that every day, all of us face change driven by globalism, competition, and the fact that technology is changing all the time. So people have to keep on learning, acquiring new knowledge and skills," explains e-learning pioneer Steve Shank, founder of Capella University (www.capella.edu), an online accredited university based in Minneapolis. "The benefits of online education are absolutely compelling," says Shank. "It's not just delivery of e-learning itself; it's also all the support services that surround the learning. The web provides a great support structure to reach out and help the individual."

Your Technology

Without getting into details, you need to determine how elaborate your technology must be to deliver the courses you plan to offer or to post the courses and programs of other education providers. Along with your web site, which will serve as your home base, you need the tools necessary to bring online education to life. This may involve a computer network, streaming video, CBT content, online chats, an online bulletin board, and of course, a means of collecting payment for course fees. Additionally, you will want to establish ways and means to interact with students and instructors to facilitate learning, answer questions, and solve disputes.

Your technologic infrastructure will have to be preplanned, blue-printed, and developed in conjunction with the technology most of your target audience has. This is very important because if your technology is too advanced, you can lose a large portion of your target market. Do not assume that everyone has the latest in computer technology; try to work within commonly found computer specifications. In other words, always work at the lower end of the curve. For example, although there has been a rapid increase in consumer wireless and broadband in the past several years, you will do yourself and your participants a disservice if you do not offer a means of downloading via dial-up.

The success of your online endeavor depends largely on establishing a very user-friendly web site from which students can select courses, seminars, CD-ROMs, or whatever it is that you offer. It also depends on maintaining that web site and making sure your online offerings do not become either obsolete or stale. Additionally, you need to use technology to market yourself through various advertising and marketing ventures, to stay one-step ahead of your competition. For example, Precision Information of Madison, Wisconsin, relies partly on a technical edge: the company's unique database structure allows for customizing content for personal finance trainers. But Precision (www.precisioninformation.com) must figure out what to do next for an encore.

More on the tech aspect of the online education world will come up later. For now, it is important that you determine how (and who) will build your site and your infrastructure. The founder of eLearners.com, C.J. DeSantis used his own knowledge of educational technology to design and build the original web site himself in 1999, with the help of college interns versed in computer technology. The site was designed to serve as a meeting point for learners and educational organizations.

Brainstorming Your Business

So which is the right niche for you? Where do you fit in? The answer depends on a confluence of factors—your location, your background, your personal preferences, your business skill set, your financing, and, of course, where you see an opportunity.

Over the next several chapters, we'll explore the state of different popular online education markets in greater depth. But those observations will still be broad strokes. The discussion is just a backdrop for your individual opportunity, which you have to determine for yourself. And you can't do that just by jumping in where the hype is loudest or even where money is being made.

Doing his business start-up research, Mark Carey, CEO of MySoftwareHelper (www.mysoftwarehelper.com), a training reseller in Tacoma, Washington, came to a crossroads where he had to decide whether to create online learning courseware or sell it. "I decided to sell e-learning as opposed to create e-learning," he says. "I'm a sales guy, not a developer. I have 18 years of sales experience."

Tip...

Smart Tip

A good source for data on the online education market research and ideas is the American Society of Training and Development (www.astd.org). Membership costs $180 a year and opens up a wealth of studies and white papers, newsletters, and bulletins.

Determining where your own personal strengths lie is a critical preliminary step prior to embarking on any new business venture. Take stock of yourself and make a list of the areas in which your skills and abilities would work best. You can also determine the areas in which you need to seek out assistance. Remember, most successful entrepreneurs have not made it without seeking out some help and/or building a team, so don't feel badly if you can't do it all yourself.

3

Start-Up Strategies

Starting a business of any kind is challenging. But the depth and breadth of an online education business is such that you should have no problem finding a niche that suits your interests and financial resources. You may start as a contractor working for a content provider, corporation, or educational institution. At the other end of the spectrum, if you have the financial resources, you might invest hundreds of thousands of dollars developing a software product or an online learning environment. Of course, most likely, you will find yourself somewhere in between.

In this chapter, we'll detail some of the most established online education opportunities, so at least you'll know the paths most traveled. It's then up to you to blaze your trail.

First off, you have to come up with the grand idea. That may be the product of a lifelong ambition. It may be the result of market research. You may be working in a related field and see an opportunity that just shouts out to you, even though no one else hears it.

Success Stories

In 1987, John Clemons, now CEO of LearnKey (www.learnkey.com) in Orem, Utah, noticed that many people were having trouble getting up to speed on a hot selling word processing package developed by another local company, WordPerfect. A producer of educational films for the Brigham Young University Motion Picture Studio at the time, Clemons decided that the world needed an educational video of a WordPerfect expert providing step-by-step instructions on the software. Clemons began taping instruction sessions in his basement and marketing them directly to WordPerfect users. Now his company has online learning partners worldwide and sells mostly to corporations.

Joe Saari, co-founder of Precision Information in Madison, Wisconsin, knew he wanted to be in business long before he knew what business he wanted to be in. It went all the way back to a childhood selling the produce from his vegetable garden door-to-door. By the time he had received his MBA in finance and was working as a consumer advisor for a large financial services company, he was positive that he didn't want to work for someone else all his life.

Saari always had several ideas incubating at any time. But his experience in the financial services industry showed him the need for a complete financial reference for experts and novices alike. Saari and his partners created a searchable *Encyclopedia of Personal Finance* online and on CD-ROM. Since 1999, Precision Information has helped more than a million people improve their understanding of financial topics.

Similarly, Sarah Chapman and Devin Williams of Spry Learning had talked about going into business together since meeting in college. Chapman graduated with degrees in economics and political science. After college, she headed up national accounts for specialty markets for one of the nation's largest book publishers. Williams collected a bachelor's degree in finance and a Harvard MBA, and became a financial analyst for a large investment banking firm.

The two wanted a business that leveraged their skills and technology and helped people. That brought them to senior centers with the idea of creating a communication device to help seniors stay in touch with their families. They soon realized that there was a real need to expand the horizons of seniors who often became landlocked in their residential communities. Chapman and Williams set up a nationwide company that helps assisted living staff teach computer basics to seniors, and then delivers courses and other services over the Net. Spry Learning is now passing $4 million in annual revenues.

C.J. DeSantis founded eLearners.com in 1999, after graduating with an MS in education a year earlier from a distance learning program from George Washington University. He was impressed by the program. He developed a concept to create a meeting place for people looking for online education courses and online course providers so consumers could find the college courses or programs that best suited their needs. Without much outside funding available at that time, CJ built the site on a bootstrap budget and managed to outlast many would-be competitors. During the first two years, he constructed a client list of about 20 schools, which were listed on a pay-on-performance basis, meaning the schools were in a no-lose situation. "Unless we delivered a qualified inquiry to them, it didn't cost them any money," explains eLearners.com CEO, Andrew Gansler.

Meanwhile, the site built a robust database of as many online educational facilities as possible and promoted the site both online and offline. "Slowly the number of paying customers increased," says Gansler. The site now lists over 2,000 programs or courses at over 130 institutions. "They pay us if they generate qualified inquiries," adds Gansler of what is now an industry leader in connecting students with online schools and courses.

Even if you follow an online education road that is well-traveled, there is always the opportunity to put your own special spin on it. To be truly successful, you must offer something unique in your approach, your marketing, your cost structure, the quality of your service, or another key aspect that sets you apart from others. Then, you need to be flexible and reinvent yourself along the way as soon as you see others jumping on your bandwagon. Remember, there is a lot of competition, so do diligent research as you proceed.

> Tip...
>
> **Smart Tip**
>
> In any business, you'll want to develop multiple revenue streams to soften any blow from changing economic conditions. For example, your primary revenue stream might be training courses. But you might also earn additional revenue by selling related products such as textbooks, software, or computer hardware.

There are a lot of different ways to get into the e-learning business. Each has pros and cons. Each requires different skills and personalities.

Each can also require vastly different amounts of start-up capital. As with any start-up scenario, it will take some time until you establish a good reputation and a network of customers. To illustrate the range of e-learning opportunities, we'll provide details on two very different kinds of businesses below, including certifying IT professionals (a well-defined and well-established approach) and acting as an online education middleman.

Filling a Certifiable Need

There is a serious skills shortage in many technical areas, and certifications are a popular way for employers to differentiate among qualified and unqualified job candidates.

"Certification is no substitute for a university degree," says Doug Kendzierski, assistant vice provost at the University of Maryland, Baltimore. "But the largest challenge for industry right now is to find a beating pulse with a propensity to succeed in a technical career track," he says. "The employment community is turning to the certification to differentiate between those with validated skills that are in the mainstream of employment, and those that are more of an employment risk." From the student's perspective, certification offers a way to get up to speed in technical areas and to break into the high-tech job market quickly with some marketable, proven skills.

While a degree in computer science may take four or more years and cost up to $100,000, a string of enabling certifications can be achieved in under six months and cost just a few thousand dollars. They can be pursued before—or more likely—after landing a job. In the latter case, it's very common for employers to pick up some or all the tab for the training.

"What you get with IT certification is some immediate bang for your buck in terms of salary increase," says Amit Yoran, professor at George Washington University in Washington, DC, and co-founder and CEO of managed security company RIPTech, which was acquired by Symantec in 2002. "It's a skill set and a criteria that a lot of employers look for when filling technical positions."

"An IT worker can't advance indefinitely without a university degree," adds Yoran. But many IT professionals pursue higher degrees

Bright Idea

Boost interest in your certification site the way they do at video arcades: Post the names of your top ten performers and the percentile scores for any student who asks. Satisfy their curiosity, and give them bragging rights and verifiable proof of excellence that they can use to enhance their prospects for promotions and new jobs.

Building Brainbench

While some organizations focus on training students to take certification exams approved by specific product vendors, others create their own certifications indicating successful completion of a course of study in a broader topic area, such as networking. Brainbench (www.brainbench.com) in Chantilly, Virginia, became the big kahuna of high-tech certifications over the Net virtually overnight. Founded by Mike Littman and two partners in 1998, Brainbench has more than a million registered users who have taken 5 million certification exams in 400 subjects.

Seeing a clear need for screening IT professionals in the workplace, Littman left the corporate world and established a web site where employers could prescreen worker knowledge levels in high-tech subjects (no training, just testing) prior to hiring.

A year later, Brainbench was hearing that its testing compared favorably to IT certifications elsewhere, so it changed its marketing strategy to target high-tech personnel. The site did 1,000 tests its first month and now provides certification exams online and at testing centers around the country for anyone who enrolls—particularly IT credential-seekers.

Brainbench works both sides of the street. Students who take its exams can make their information public, giving potential employers an opportunity to search the Brainbench database for a short list of job candidates. For example, an employer could go in and find the top 10 percent of people who passed a network administration course in a city or state.

after certifications have already landed them jobs. Fortunately, even advanced degrees can be achieved online now—and often in much less time than through traditional universities. In the meantime, employers generally recognize certifications as adequate evidence of technical achievement, and additional certifications usually lead to higher salaries and increased responsibilities.

Certification courses provide the ad hoc training high-tech pros need and are necessary for the growth and advancement of even those who hold computer-related degrees. Employers want people with highly specialized skills that are not necessarily available at the university. A certification proves to a potential employer that a candidate has a specific set of proven skills or knows how to operate a certain software package or hardware platform.

Certifiably Different

Certification facilities traditionally ran in brick-and-mortar classrooms. But increasingly, both certification training and testing are being delivered online—either synchronously or asynchronously or in combination. (For some courses, self-paced online training must be augmented with hands-on classroom sessions.)

Unlike skill training, which focuses on teaching a student how to use a particular application or do a specific task such as run a network, exam training is a cram session. Although the theoretical goal is the same—to teach a student a level of proficiency in a given subject—the end result of certification training is the ability to pass the exam and gain the certification. Training is, therefore, usually very focused.

> Tip...
>
> **Smart Tip**
>
> To certify others, you must be certified yourself. In the vendor-specific area, for example, Microsoft offers several trainer designations. Vendor-specific training is highly competitive. For vendor-neutral training, CompTIA has its CTT+ certification. This designation shows that a technical instructor has gained a standard of excellence in training and is well-versed in at least one topic. Vendor-neutral training may offer more avenues because you are not tied to a single vendor, allowing you more flexibility against the competition.

Actually giving the exams is another potential business opportunity. You can focus on two types of certifications: vendor-neutral and vendor-specific. A vendor-specific certification prepares a student to understand and operate a specific vendor's technology. A vendor-neutral certification, on the other hand, goes more into the underlying theory behind the specific technology. If you have a vendor-neutral background, it becomes much easier to move among corporate clients who may have different technologies in place. Both certifications have value, both are popular, and some people prefer to take both.

Starting any kind of certification center requires a larger-than-average investment in infrastructure, especially if you need facilities for classroom training. Considering the physical plant, trained personnel, and high-level content, you could easily spend $250,000 to get started. But your chances of success are good.

Making a Middleman Market

Many entrepreneurs are consummate deal makers, and that puts them in position to be great middlemen. Rather than running an online training center, you can be the middle person that puts students into classes offered at various schools, much as eLearners.com does. As a facilitator, your online educational business can match students not only with specific online courses but also with consultants and products—from CD-ROMS to text books—to support the educational needs of the student.

Offering a one-stop shop on the web is nothing new. Every market needs people devoted to supporting the smooth flow of information and business transactions among different levels of service providers and their customers. In the parlance of the internet at large, there are B2B and B2C revenue models, and middlemen support both. In education, there are so many different courses and categories of courses, so many training organizations and certification bodies, so many prices and options to discover that consumers can easily feel overwhelmed. They may not know what sort of training and certification they really need, where to start looking, or how to differentiate between providers. The source of that guidance may take many forms: a phone-book-size printed guide, a specialized web search engine, an online learning portal, a course broker, or various combinations of the above.

> **Tip...**
>
> **Smart Tip**
>
> While the prices of IT courses vary widely, there are no clearly definable differences in profitability for the trainer of a vendor-specific course or a vendor-neutral content. Most IT workers need both types of training for their resumes. Therefore, for maximum traffic, offer a mixture of both.

WorldWideLearn (www.WorldWideLearn.com) also functions as a one-stop shop for electronic education for individual students. The site provides information resources as well as links to hundreds of online courses in over 100 subject categories—everything from a Ph.D. to courses on wireless technologies, sales training, and aromatherapy. The menu is broad, but the company specializes in matching students to online universities and certification courses.

You're never limited to just one learning opportunity, and sometimes those who provide directory or brokerage services teach as well. OneOnOne Computer Training (www.oootraining.com), a veteran computer training company in Addison, Illinois, hawks its own set of courseware, but it concentrates on bringing parties together, negotiating deals, and earning fees in the process. Founded in 1976 by Lee McFadden to publish self-paced math instruction for schools, the business has evolved into a provider of quick tips and just-in-time tutorials on different aspects of popular productivity software to thousands of office workers. It also offers more complex IT training courses in conjunction with online partners.

DevX (www.devx.com) offers online training, but is more of an omnibus source of information and training resources for the IT community, with newsletters, libraries, chat rooms, bulletin boards, and a variety of media. The Palo Alto, California, firm maintains a database/online exchange of 30,000 IT white papers and various service providers. Additionally, DevX develops custom web portals through which corporations can deliver just-in-time e-learning, expert tips, code libraries, collaboration tools, and premium content and services to their employees.

Of course, you can always narrow down your web offerings to meet the needs of a specific industry. NAPA Auto Parts, for example, is a car parts manufacturer and operator of the nationwide chain of more than 6,000 auto parts stores and 11,000 NAPA service centers. It also happens to operate a very sophisticated online learning center. The NAPA Institute for Automotive Technology (www.niat-training.com) conducts online training sessions for local repair shop staffers and independent automotive technicians annually. The site operates in conjunction with NAPA's long-running classroom training program. While NAPA has the benefits of being in the auto parts business, you can utilize an industry or business that is familiar to you and provide such training, or work in conjunction with an established business. Being the educational arm of a large corporation can be both profitable and provide you with steady financing.

It's Who You Know

Part of your decision when contemplating which road to follow will come down to the resources and contacts you are able to establish. Whether you are seeking instructors to provide original course content, online educational providers in order for you to serve as a middleman, consultants or manufacturers of educational software products, you need to establish relationships. Not unlike most e-commerce businesses, many of which are dependant on vendors and fulfillment houses, you need to start making connections with educational institutions.

The idea of building a network should factor into your initial start-up plan. How good are you at networking? Schmoozing? Selling? To offer courses from 50, 60, or 70 institutions, you need to interact with someone in a decision-making capacity at each school or university. Likewise, to market courses for certification, you need to meet with the certification board in a specific field or executives at software companies. Selling products or services almost always involves building relationships. You need to establish contacts at the start of your business venture and expand them as your business grows.

To begin, determine how far-reaching you plan to stretch your business. Are you looking for a few good instructors or 100 online universities from around the world? No matter which is the path for you, it is imperative from the beginning that you immerse yourself in the

> **Bright Idea**
> Once you are off and running, ask every customer for a testimonial, and post these testimonials from satisfied customers on your web site.

online educational field. Along with seeking information online, you should start attending seminars, symposiums, conferences, and other gatherings of educators, administrators, and those who could be good connections once you get the business off the ground. Learn about the field, meet the players, and keep track of all information as you do your due diligence. You need to be well-versed in the online education field before venturing into it.

4

Online Education Goes to School

Online education has made huge inroads in the classic learning centers: K–12 schools and colleges. E-learning also plays an ever-greater role in the fast-growing homeschooling movement.

Online education has become most visible publicly in colleges. Traditional colleges and community colleges are deep into e-learning, and the online or virtual college has gained surprising popularity. These institutions are both competition and partners for online education entrepreneurs. Even if you aren't starting your own electronic college, the ones in existence can be customers for your content or software. Likewise, college campuses offer resources to entrepreneurs—classrooms, student connections, and marketing vehicles. In this chapter, we'll look at opportunities in schools, starting with elementary and secondary schools and move up the line to colleges.

e-Writing, e-Reading, e-Arithmetic

"The United States has done a pretty good job populating K–12 classrooms and libraries with computers. But there is a disconnect between the hardware and the children who use it," says the Pew Internet & American Life Project, which recently studied the interaction between kids and computers.

Pew gives schools an F in designing coursework and in providing computer usage basics. The same teens and preteens who can handle a joystick better than an F-14 fighter pilot have trouble in efficiently navigating both the computer and the internet. One big problem, reports Pew, is that they haven't learned to touch-type. Another is that while they may be expert at certain computer skills like downloading MP3 audio files, there are vast gaps in their knowledge of "useful" computer skills and features.

On an up note, schools are gaining more of the latest technologies, including laptops, wireless networks, and DVD drives. The problem is, while there are more computers at school, getting sufficient screen time is something else again. Middle school and high school students move from place to place and from teacher to teacher during the school day. Only a brief period is spent with access to internet-connected computers. While vastly improved in recent years, the student-to-computer ratio is still 4 to 1, according to MDR.

Additionally, research activities often are stymied by policies designed to protect kids. The federal Children's Internet Protection Act often restricts access and blocks content. Unfortunatly, as the internet remains largely unmonitored, children need to be more protected today than ever on all computers, at school and at home, where unmonitored internet access has led to some horrific stories.

It doesn't take major studies by research groups, however, to see that kids today are very interested in computer use, much to the dismay of some TV network programming heads, who find themselves losing viewers to the computers, with their interactive possibilities. Today, more than three out of four high school and middle school students use the internet regularly. While most teens and preteens use it primarily for social interactions and entertainment purposes, sometimes these students actually use it to research school assignments, confer with classmates, and get papers completed.

This combination of at-home access and keen interest in the internet makes young people excellent candidates for online learning. But how can you replace video games, My Space, and Aim with learning? How do you keep kids interested in educational offerings?

Bright Idea

Why not mix education with pleasure? Start an internet cafe targeted at teens doing homework. Don't forget to offer some supervision and take some sensible precautions.

One way is by linking them with hands-on activities, which fits well with the latest educational thinking. According to a study by Rockman et al (www.rockman.com), a technology and consulting firm, elementary school students learn better when teachers link curriculum to hands-on projects—building models, designing buildings, or depicting living environments. Students are better able to visualize and assimilate a wide variety of subjects—not just science and social studies but also math and language arts—if they feel that they are "discovering" knowledge rather than repeating it. As an entrepreneur, you can achieve this with interactive educational activities that incorporate an element of fun.

Among successful players in the K–12 market, LearnStar (www.learnstar.com) in Dallas partnered with local computer resellers to bring laptops and wireless networks to elementary schools. The payoff is the interactive, quiz-style activities that LearnStar has designed to enhance learning, increase student motivation, and according to the company, increase students' standardized test scores by nearly 38 percent.

Kumon math and reading centers (www.kumon.com) in Teaneck, New Jersey, which offers supplemental after-school education from more than 1,300 franchise locations nationwide, offers a blend of online learning and more traditional methods to teach the youngest children reading readiness skills. That includes listening to reading CDs, games using alphabet boards, posters to sound out letters, singing, and flash cards.

America's schoolchildren need help with math, reading, and other things they need to know. And where there's a vacuum this size, entrepreneurs will fill it. Family Education Network also offers a couple of online learning sites for kids. Rekids.com provides interactive and fun learning activities for the K–12 audience. Educational games, projects, and homework help are all included. FunBrain.com is a site that is set up to involve kids, parents, and teachers in the learning process. While these sites are under the umbrella of a larger company, the concept of providing interactive, entertaining learning activities for kids of all ages is a distinct possibility for a new online education entrepreneur. Remember, online learning does not require a classroom setting or a standard course curriculum. It is very important, however, to work with someone (or a team) with an education background to assure that you are providing challenging material at the right grade levels.

Homes Rule!

Nearly two million students are being homeschooled throughout the United States today. It's a grassroots reaction to declining test scores in public schools, local increases in violence and drug use, and concerns about peer pressure and mass culture. While the debate goes on about whether these students suffer in learning social skills, the reality is that homeschooling opens up additional opportunities for entrepreneurs. Who supplies the course materials for homeschooling? How do parents get trained to school their kids? Who helps them with academic record-keeping, college, and career counseling for their teens, and issues like discipline and fostering peer interaction with other kids? A web site such as homeschool.com (www.homeschool.com) serves as a gateway to all sorts of information and links to everything related to schooling children at home.

Bright Idea

The Craft and Hobby Industry Association offers educational project sheets with materials to help you incorporate hands-on projects into coursework in the "Teacher Place" section of its web site. You could also provide such hands-on learning projects for home schoolers.

Colleges accept homeschooled youngsters, but they may have additional hoops to jump through. Who will help them? Jones International University (www.jonesinternational.edu) in Chicago, a fully accredited online university that lets homeschooled students take college-level courses prior to high school graduation.

The National Home Education Research Institute and various other nonprofit support groups provide curricula and other help for parents who choose to homeschool. However, these groups hold no monopoly on the activity. It's like other areas

Head of the Board

The Blackboard Learning System from Blackboard Inc. (www.blackboard.com) in Washington, DC, is a fixture on many college campuses as well as in corporations and some K–12 classrooms as well. An interactive learning environment with bulletin board, e-mail server, and chat room, Blackboard enhances the classroom experience and streamlines academic logistics.

Among other benefits, such "course management systems," Blackboard and rival, eCollege (recognized for its innovative technology and smart business model), offer learning products, online services, communities, and much more.

of business; people develop a level of expertise and use their skills to guide others. While there are educational requirements to be met, homeschooling is ripe with possibilities for the determined online educational entrepreneur.

Type "homeschooling" or "home schooling" into any internet search engine and you will turn up a wealth of homeschooling web portals that can tell you everything you need to know about the subject and give you a few moneymaking ideas. Think about it: Who would be more amenable to downloading online educational content or resources than parents who are homeschooling their children? You can deliver courses or other resources for kids, give elementary education classes for parents, publish a homeschooling e-zine or newsletter, run a homework chat room, or establish a web portal for other homeschooling service providers.

Online Education and the College Campus

Post-secondary online education is still dominated by traditional colleges and universities. After all, they've pretty much owned the education franchise for a few hundred years. But that's slowly changing. The market is opening up in no small part because education no longer has to be restricted to being "on campus." Demand for college level (and postgraduate) education is outstripping the ability of the traditional educational establishment to build new campus facilities or to support the number of students crowding onto the campuses they now have. The disparity is particularly acute among state-funded colleges and universities, especially the nation's 1,100 community colleges, which often must accept all students who apply without commensurate budget increases.

If you think about it, it is easy to find colleges in the United States that have stood for well over 100 years. However, try finding colleges that opened their doors in the past 10 to 20 years. There are perhaps a handful of new colleges in the United States, which means the established universities must accommodate the growing percentage of high school graduates that now go on to college.

Combine the steady growth of online college enrollees with the vast number of people pursuing other types of continuing education—everything from traffic school to the pursuit of a hobby to pursuing professional certifications—and you

Stat Fact

Most colleges and universities today (more than 84 percent) operate a distance learning program, with nearly half these schools offering accredited degrees over the internet, according to market research firm Market Data Retrieval.

have a tremendous population of learners that the classic school environment can no longer handle. The proliferation of online universities and other e-learning ventures is proof of that. The University of Phoenix Online (www.uop .edu–info.com) alone claims more than 50,000 students in the United States.

Fun Fact

Not only are 100 percent of colleges and universities connected to the internet but also 64 percent of classrooms are connected, according to market research firm Market Data Retrieval.

Traditional universities tend to focus first on young adults by providing extension or community outreach programs and second on extending their charter to include older learners in the vicinity. Many of the electronic colleges, or online arms of traditional colleges, are now also reaching out to working adults.

A certain segment of the population postpones higher education in favor of entering the work force after high school. Others are forced out of college early to meet family financial needs. Additionally, many adult learners are college graduates who for business or personal reasons want to return for additional college level courses, for credit or not. Adult learners typically have time constraints that teens and 20-somethings don't: full-time jobs and families. Online learning in general can help by eliminating travel time and offering a broader, more flexible schedule.

Today, there is practically no college-level class to which online education techniques cannot be applied. It would be hard to imagine a bachelor of science program nowadays in which computers are not central. Bachelor of arts programs lag only a little. In fact, it's the rare subject in the traditional brick-and-mortar campus, in the social sciences or even fine arts, that doesn't involve some internet research. Many add multimedia tools, teacher-to-student e-mail, or internet chat sessions, or the use of web sites for posting class information, curricula, or lectures.

Colleges have invested heavily in infrastructure for computer usage. The difference, however, is that in recent years, the use of the computer and the internet has gone from a supplementary role to the driving force behind much education. Students today are doing more than using the internet as a supplement to the traditional classroom. They are signing up for virtual courses that begin by going online and sometimes continue with virtual classrooms.

No one has to tell a student how a computer can help smooth the path to a degree. This is the post-Nintendo generation, and most grew up with a game controller in their hands and access to a computer at home or school. A recent Pew Internet & American Life Project survey found that one-fifth of college students first started using computers between the ages of 5 and 8. By age 18, all had used one.

Bottom line: You don't have to sell students on the benefits of learning by computer. But how do you focus on the segment you want to reach, and how will you reach them?

Who's in the Audience?

Whether you are targeting college-age students in traditional institutions or jobholders working toward a bachelor's or advanced degree, the audience is relatively affluent. And if some people lack extra money, loans, scholarship, and employers can help.

The 15 million-plus U.S. college students aged 18 to 30 have discretionary buying power of nearly $200 billion a year, according to one 360 Youth/Harris Interactive College Explorer Study. (360 Youth is a youth marketing group, while Harris Interactive is a leading web market research company). Parents and scholarships also help with tuition. And, an increase in both programs and eligibility for loans and/or scholarships has opened the doors to students from more varied financial backgrounds. For employees returning to school, employers are often only too happy to underwrite an employee's continuing education because it enhances his or her role in the workplace. You are also now looking at a working audience, with regular earnings, taking online courses.

There is, therefore, a market that is deep and broad. The people who populate it have one thing in common—a limited amount of time to get the job done. Online education, particularly distance learning, offers a new level of flexibility and the chance to optimize time, the most precious commodity for adult learners.

Generation Internet

Today's college kids are more sophisticated about technology than any previous generation. They are well-equipped with PCs and other devices, have demonstrated knowledge about them, and have strong preferences for certain brands. Ninety-two percent own a computer and many have handheld computers. According to a recent 360 Youth/Harris Interactive College Explorer Study, approximately 93 percent of the 15.6 million U.S. college students aged 18 to 30 access the internet regularly, making them the most connected segment of the population. They are quick to invest in new technologies, with two-thirds of students interviewed saying they are either among the first to buy a new gadget or device, or will buy soon after seeing their peers try it.

College students have a relatively large amount of free time that could be used to advance their education. Including weekends, they have an average of 11 hours per day of unscheduled time when they're not sleeping, working, studying, or attending class, reports the Harris Interactive Study. But schoolwork does not necessarily drive their interest in technology (big surprise!).

When you examine how young adults use the internet, the themes of recreation and communication sound loud and clear. College students are frequently found talking on their cell phones, and when they aren't actually talking, they are text messaging one another or communicating via e-mail or instant messenger. Additionally, they do use the computers often bought by mom and/or dad for research, reports, and gathering various materials for coursework.

So Are They Ready for Internet Courses?

To date, only a small portion of college students (less than 10 percent) are taking courses by internet, and half of the students who took an online course believed they learned less from the online course than they would have from the classroom experience. That is, however, good news for you: It means that the market is barely penetrated, and current providers may not be doing an adequate job of selling the online educational experience. Sure, it is hard to beat the socialization of in-person classes for college students who spend a portion of class time checking each other out. And, it's unlikely that online education will have the administrators of major halls of learning shutting their doors. But, if you could channel one of the five courses on each student's schedule into an online course to better fit in with his or her busy social calendar and off-campus job, you could make a fortune.

The key is to infiltrate the college learning experience, rather than trying to replace it. As high tech as the younger generation may be, there is still only a small percentage of students who will opt for the full online college experience over "being there."

Of course, to work in conjunction with a college or university, you need to demonstrate that you will be providing an online experience that meets the same high standards as traditional courses. This includes a presentation of your course outline, structure, curriculum, how you plan to deliver the courses, and who will serve as instructors. It also includes the key areas of how students will be motivated and how testing will be handled to assure integrity. Often, when working with a college or university, the online course culminates with testing in a traditional classroom setting, whether that is on campus or off. More on preparing courses will be discussed in Chapter 7.

The Other College "Kids"

Not everyone finishes college in their early 20s. There are a lot of back-to-schoolers working at companies while looking to complete their undergraduate and graduate degrees. If you choose to target the back-to-college demographic, you will be addressing a more worldly audience, one that has less time on its hands and needs the convenience and flexibility that you can offer. Therefore, you need to make "ease of scheduling" a priority, which typically means leaning toward asynchronous learning.

Stat Fact

According to the National Center for Educations Statistics, the fastest-growing group attending higher education institutions are working, part-time students older than 25, termed *learning adults* or *adult learners*.

The most common reasons for not completing college typically include the fixed hours of institutional learning, prohibitive attendance requirements, lack of child care or other family support, and unfocused course information. Solving these problems creates a huge potential opportunity.

Conspicuously absent from that list is financial problems. Now, money is always a problem to some degree, but there are untold millions of dollars offered by companies for underwriting education that are going unused. NCES surveys indicate that 95 percent of U.S. employees with education benefits tied to their employment don't take advantage of this opportunity. Part of the reason is that students usually have to pay tuition up front and are only reimbursed by their companies.

But the principal problem for these students is time. Interestingly, of the 5 percent of workers who do take advantage of company educational benefits, says NCES, more than 85 percent now pursue their education at least partly online.

While NCES studies show that college-age students are taking ever longer to get their degrees, working students are all about getting it done. Who wouldn't be when working days and going to school nights and on weekends?

Don't forget those serving their country, a huge and highly motivated group. Saint Leo University (www.saintleo.edu) in Saint Leo, Florida, claims to be the largest provider of complete online degree programs for the U.S. Army, with more than 38,000 enrolled in 14 regional centers on military bases and at community colleges—and that's just one branch of service. American Military University (www.amu.edu) is an education provider for military personnel online. More than 15,000 students from 30 countries, mostly holding positions in various branches of the United States military, take its online courses.

Follow the Money

Colleges and universities are a massive market for online education. MDR says that colleges continue to increase their spending on hardware, software, and a wide range of technology-related services, and that spending now runs over $5 billion annually.

> **Bright Idea**
>
> Don't miss the opportunity that a fast-growing Hispanic community offers to specialize in Spanish-language online educational opportunities.

"Course management systems, which provide a common user interface for professors to construct and deliver courses, are commonplace on college campuses, where wireless networks have also become very common in recent years. Content and teaching time aren't the only things entrepreneurs can offer colleges. Someone needs to provide, and keep providing, those course management systems (CMS), which make it easy for instructors to construct and deliver online courses.

Some of the most popular CMSs come from Blackboard (www.blackboard.com) and eCollege (www.ecollege.com). They offer the infrastructure required to deliver courses with all the necessary features (such as bulletin boards) in a well-integrated user interface. They also can simplify integration into the institution's own systems for online registration, grade reporting, and other administration tasks. CMSs, which are also used extensively in corporate and even in K–12 education, can be bought with existing courses.

This aspect of online education, designing and building the learning infrastructure, is a business opportunity for those with a technical background and the vision to create a fast, effective, and user-friendly means of learning. While the courses and front-end (what the consumer sees) educational offerings need to be unique from one learning institution to another, the methods of communication, or the back-end infrastructure, can be the same. It's not unlike several very distinctive restaurants serving entirely different styles of cuisine, but all using the same leading brand of kitchen appliances. You're providing the appliances, or applications in this case.

To your advantage, your market is not limited to the creation and development of new online learning establishments, but spills over into the area of upgrading and improving upon the systems out there that have already been implemented. Therefore, if you can create a faster, more efficient, user-friendly means of delivering course content to students, you can then market your product to learning institutions that are not up-to-speed or have room for improvement. There is a lot of money to be made in the technical area of online education. You just need to know that there is stiff competition from the developers of such back-end technology.

For those with a production background, there is also the producing end of online courses. When the internet first took off in the late 1990s, many would-be and even some successful television producers and directors jumped over to the internet. Of course, many were designing entertainment-based web sites, most of which were not well-received, but there were others designing online courses. Producing and marketing packaged courses or custom-designed courses for online

Doing a Bisk Business

What's the biggest name on the virtual campus? Yale? Harvard? Phoenix? How about Bisk Education (www.bisk.com)? Nope, the Tampa, Florida, company hasn't appeared in any New Year's Day bowl games. But because of the consortium of online universities it has built (www.universityalliance.com), this e-venture can claim to be one of the nation's largest providers of accredited online college degree programs. Among the universities participating in Bisk's University Alliance are St. Leo, Regis, Tulane, and Florida Tech. Bisk works extensively with *Fortune* 500 companies, which are more than willing to underwrite the continuing education of their employees. Students have been recruited from American Airlines, Boeing, Dell, FedEx, Home Depot, Hewlett-Packard, NASA, and Sony Music Entertainment.

Founded in 1971 by Nathan Bisk, the online educational technology includes streaming video and audio lectures, which you can view as many times as you like, as well as virtual office hours in chat rooms where students can discuss lectures with their instructors. Web pages are used for displaying a syllabus, weekly assignments, and grades. Student interaction is fostered with chat rooms, message boards, and e-mail.

learning is another business angle. Global Education Network (GEN.com) spent hours and many dollars to have its inhouse producers and course developers work with professors at various colleges to develop high-tech courses. And, they worked with these producers and highly dedicated computer techies to make sure the back-end structure supported the courses. Unfortunatly GEN.com subsequently disappeared because it forgot one little thing—marketing. But that's a whole other story. The point is, that you can make money with a business designing/producing online courses.

As CMSs expand their functionality, they start to turn into learning management systems (LMSs), which are sometimes described as complete "ecosystems" for online education. These systems integrate CMS with other software tools for solving all the learning needs of an enterprise (educational or other). Again, a college may want help in acquiring, setting up, and running an LMS or upgrading (or replacing) its current LMS.

Some institutions are moving a limited number of classes to a distance learning format as pilot programs, while others are going full-speed ahead with degree programs, many at the graduate level, that can be delivered to students at remote locations.

Obviously, electronic colleges like Jones University and University of Phoenix Online are in this latter camp. They are pushing distance learning to the limit. They also may reach out beyond knowledge workers. Jones, for example, has an outreach program to provide advanced placement to homeschooled teens. As always, there are no walls in entrepreneurship.

5

Tuning Up Knowledge Workers and IT Professionals

Training corporate workers and providing courseware or a teaching platform to corporate training programs is a huge market. Businesses have obvious training needs, they can afford to pay substantially, and they typically buy in volume. A license for hundreds of seats for just one course isn't unusual, according to the people behind LearnKey of Orem, Utah, whose reseller franchisees carry its broad menu of courseware to corporations around the world and in some cases offer support and training. Competition is fierce in this market. It requires a high degree of polish, solid financing, strong sales and marketing skills, and the ability to deal with long sales cycles. In this chapter, we talk about corporate training.

Thinking Corporate

Corporate opportunities vary. You can train workers on general business skills, management techniques, applications, and processes that are unique to their industry or their company, and/or in general use of computers and computer software. There is also a very large and very well-established market for specialized training for IT professionals, which we also cover in this chapter.

John Dalton, a senior analyst at Forrester Research, interviewed 40 training managers and chief knowledge officers at Global 2500 companies. "Of those 40, 39 already had online training initiatives up and running," Dalton reports. "They're completely jazzed about it, primarily because it saves them money." One reason you can be jazzed about business training is that the delivery mechanisms can be quite sophisticated in corporations. Most companies have robust desktop equipment, high-speed internet connections, and IT pros on staff to handle tech support—which you should also provide.

Given traffic congestion, the cost of providing office space and other amenities, and the performance-orientation of knowledge worker jobs, many enlightened companies are happy to allow their workers to work from home, that is, telecommute. The right home environment is often one of the best places to get real work done. In fact, many companies provide the computing equipment and broadband DSL or cable-modem connections for their off-site employees. "The level of investment in America's remote work force is expected to increase steadily over the coming years," says Kneko Burney, an InStat director. This is in response to the need to maintain current workers rather than spending more money to find and train new ones.

Beware!

You'll market to senior staff, but you won't have the account long if students don't report back their enthusiastic approval, and management doesn't see improvement in their skills. Make sure to get student feedback, monitor their results, and check in with the client to make sure that you are meeting its needs. After all, you want to teach what your client wants its employees to learn.

As an online education entrepreneur you need to be ready to serve the telecommuting segment of the work force, which means having some alternatives for those people who are not yet up to speed with the latest technology, such as streaming media and various kinds of audio conferencing and videoconferencing. Keep in mind that your audience will vary from dial-up modems to the latest in wireless communications, so respond accordingly and have tech help trained to deal with a wide range of possible scenarios.

Looking Out for the Bottom Line

One of the biggest trends in U.S. business during the past two decades is outsourcing services. Despite sloughing off millions of employees, the *Fortune* 1000 still need to handle the same workloads. This provided a jump-start for many newly unemployed entrepreneurs, whose firms began doing basically the same tasks for their former employers, on an outsourcing basis.

Over the past ten years, outsourcing became the answer for many large corporations that were looking to trim payroll while still getting the work done. Outsourcing, while not always a popular solution with the American work force, does make economic sense. In most cases, whatever a full-time employee earns, his employer has to pay another 40 percent or so of that salary in health benefits, insurance, retirement, and other expenses. That doesn't include general and administrative costs such as office space, desks, computers, heat, light, and supplies, all of which can be substantial. Outsourcing allows businesses to essentially hire "as needed" personnel in various businesses. For example, a fully-staffed graphics department may be underutilized, but still receive full-time salaries and benefits. A corporation today can outsource its graphics material, as necessary, to a graphics design house to save money. It also allows for specialized work from professionals with expertise in the necessary area, while also saving the company money.

In the same vein, companies are eager to outsource employee training. While necessary, it is typically viewed as a cost center and an area that external firms can handle very effectively. Why does this matter to you? Just like the graphics company, you can be the business to which companies turn, only in this case, it is for education and training.

What Knowledge Workers Need to Know

What do knowledge workers need to know? The short answer is "everything." Training opportunities run the gamut from building better spreadsheets to meeting regulatory guidelines to management skills. Companies increasingly want help designing and implementing courses that are unique to their firms, whether it has to do with their specific products or their specific processes.

Naturally, courses in the whole panoply of computer skills are central to knowledge workers. A familiarity with popular applications such as Microsoft Word and PowerPoint is basically a prerequisite today for filling any job with opportunities for advancement. Of course, your business needs to stay up on the latest in technological advancement—or even be one step ahead.

There is also a growing concern about, and subsequent need for, customer relations training, as the American consumer has begun to rise up and say loudly, "We're not going to take it anymore." Shoddy service, poorly made products, unreliable tech support, and overall rudeness has consumers fuming.

> Tip...
>
> **Smart Tip**
>
> Think about professional niches for corporate workers. For instance, RedVector.com focuses on the building and design trades with courses geared toward architects, builders, and contractors. Offering more than 1,000 online courses, it works closely with businesses and universities to ensure that all courses are approved or registered with state boards and professional organizations.

Time management, productivity, communication skills, and project management are among the areas where corporate training is now big business. Therefore, if you can provide the online educational tools for corporations to outsource, then you can fill a niche in the market. Of course, you will need to have instructors and courses that cover these areas inside and out—and are up-to-date.

Teach the Web on the Web

What better than the electronic media to teach workers how to use the electronic media? Virtually overnight, workplaces have been transformed into electronic information warehouses, and the internet and messaging have become unavoidable aspects of every knowledge worker's daily grind. A growing number of people are interested in learning how to do things that once might have been considered restricted to professionals, such as web page design and web site optimization. They may need specific information about systems such as CRM (customer resource management) and ERP (electronic resource procurement) that are now reached through the web. Many of the big-name vendors that are providing the infrastructure for these activities are also dipping their big toes into

> **Dollar Stretcher**
>
> With small groups, try using one of the free instant messaging services to conduct ad hoc classroom discussion sessions online.

> **Beware!**
> While much of the subject matter might appear standard, companies contracting for employee training aren't likely to be satisfied with canned courses. They'll usually have individual requirements that necessitate at least some customization of popular topics.

online education—including Cisco, Hewlett-Packard, IBM, Oracle, PeopleSoft, SAP, Siebel Systems, and Sun Microsystems. James Lundy, a vice president and research director at Gartner, an IT consulting firm, points to the entry of such big fish as a signal that online learning has become mainstream.

Today, in an age where business travel has become more time-consuming and expensive, both employees and corporate managers would prefer to find alternatives to paying for air travel to conferences, seminars, and training sessions in other parts of the country. Online education is a solution, particularly to small and medium-sized companies that lack the budget to send employees off-site. However, you can't conduct effective training seminars to employees based in 35 different locations from the comfort of your office without learning how to do so. And so, a course on how to utilize the internet for employee training is born.

Custom Coursework

In addition to broad-based computer, business, and management courses, a growing number of your potential customers will want courses unique to them. These often go beyond the usual knowledge worker productivity applications. Many have to do with special proprietary software or equipment that the company uses, or are task-related. Some topics will be unique to a company, or companies may ask that it be delivered in a unique way that speaks to the company's mission.

Over the years, MiraCosta College, in Oceanside, California, has developed a core of 50 or so classes on popular topics such as English as a Second Language and the standard supervisory skills. When these don't suffice, a MiraCosta representative meets with the company and assesses its needs, makes a proposal, then adjusts it to the company's wishes. "We aren't here to present some predigested course," says Levy. "We're here to find out what a business needs and adapt our coursework to that need. Sometimes, that means adapting off-the-shelf coursework. But over the years, for example, we've developed a customer service course that we do differently than others."

By having custom-made courses utilizing a template (so as not to have to re-create the wheel every time), you can work closely with your clients and build an ongoing relationship that can last for years.

Training the Information Professional

There is always a great opportunity in providing courses to IT professionals such as programmers, network administrators, and web page designers. This training could be in asynchronous self-study courses over the Net or synchronous classes delivered via videoconferencing technologies and augmented by forums, scheduled chat rooms, and other communication methods. Obviously, you can assume a high level of computer competence among this audience. Ditto for motivation, especially since the IT employment market has become increasingly competitive with career paths clearly based on certification.

Taking the Long View

"The single biggest obstacle that community and technical colleges face is the ability to train faculty on the software the industry is currently using," says Bruce Brooks, director of Community Affairs for Microsoft. "Typically, there is an 18- to 24-month lag time between the time new technology is introduced in the marketplace and its adoption into academia." That's a market window likely to get wider. The technology wheel keeps turning and retraining never ends. New programming languages, new protocols, new standards, and new customer support systems are being created all the time. In a sense, the next generation of IT professionals are today's IT workers who haven't yet learned the skills they'll need to exploit technologies not yet born.

According to the U.S. Bureau of Labor Statistics, computer-related jobs will continue to experience phenomenal growth through 2010.

Remember to keep a broad view of IT needs—most notably, corporations also need training for their technical support people. Gene Kansas, from Help Desk 2000, the certification arm of IT services firm Support Technologies (www.teamstc.com), notes that "the more that people use technology, the more problems that are going to crop up. And the more problems, the more support that's needed. As technology increases, so will the demand for educated, certified people to handle it."

A job in the call center is a definite "foot in the door," adds Melissa Doble, recruiter from recruitment agency TMP Worldwide, and this "can grow into an even more technical position." Therefore, the entrepreneur whose

Tip...

Smart Tip

What jobs will be in demand in your corner of the online education market? The U.S. Bureau of Labor Statistics (www.bls.gov/opub/ooq/ooqhome.htm) details growth in 270 different IT occupations through 2010.

online education business trains the "tech support" voice at the end of the line for the multitude of high tech products, including not only computers but also security and home multimedia systems, is likely to have great success.

Home service integration is a growing market and courses that train such integrators and keep them up-to-date on the latest advances can prove very profitable. Just like IT training, mutlimedia integration and networking require ongoing training as the technology continues to evolve.

Playing It Safe

Another IT macro trend that will be with us for a long time is the need for improved security against attacks at all levels. Skilled programmers and other high-tech workers—network administrators, help desk people, and other support staff—are constantly trying to stay one step ahead of those who are hacking, phishing, and creating new methods of procuring protected data. As such threats keep growing, demand for information security personnel seems assured. Learning risk assessment, infrastructure security, and how to handle a system attack are all ongoing areas of focus for numerous IT professionals.

One of the fastest-growing certifications in IT is Certified Information Systems Security Professional (CISSP), the "gold standard" in cyber security credentials. It is offered by the International Information Systems Security Certification Consortium (ISC). The CISSP examination consists of 250 multiple choice questions, covering topics such as Access Control Systems, Cryptography, and Security Management Practices. In addition to coursework and exams, the CISSP credential requires four years experience in information security (or three years plus a bachelor's degree) and successful completion of the CISSP exam.

Beware!

Software vendors could turn out to be your business partners upon whom you may depend for coursework, certification standards, or referrals. But maintain your objectivity with savvy high-tech students or some of the shrapnel from bad software installations could fly your way.

Did We Mention Certifications?

Whatever an IT pro knows, he or she must prove it with a piece of paper to get a job or move up in the job arena. Career advancement requires the right course history. So be ready to provide certificates of completion that students can use as resume builders. Those may or may not differ from the certifications product vendors provide as the result of exam completion, depending on your business relationship with those vendors and whether you just do training or you do testing as well.

There are literally thousands of course topics, many offered by or in conjunction with product manufacturers. Others are offered by professional associations, computer resellers, or other distribution organizations, news outlets, colleges, and other traditional learning institutions. And many, of course, are presented by online education companies.

Most certificates are offered in cooperation with product providers like Cisco, which has its own networking academy, or Microsoft, which employs two independent testing companies for its certifications. These companies have established a very deep infrastructure of coursework, certification standards, and district staff to support networks of teaching partners who themselves must undergo rigorous and expensive training, be tested and certified, and demonstrate certain financial and professional qualifications.

For example, Oracle sponsors its own Oracle University and also has recognized hundreds of training organizations around the world and authorized them to deliver coursework developed through Oracle University. Similarly, Microsoft operates no less than six programs through which different kinds of training partners can become certified to offer Microsoft training and certifications.

These software makers have to ensure that the support network that they are creating delivers the best and most consistent information possible and the highest level of customer service consistent with profit. As part of a network, you'll be expected to adhere to a minimum set of standards recognized by the manufacturer as representing mastery in different products.

To earn or renew your Microsoft Certified Trainer (MCT) certification, someone in your organization must hold at least one current Microsoft certification, attend a Microsoft MCT course at a Microsoft training center, demonstrate instructional skills, and have broad technical knowledge. Then Microsoft requires you to

Smart Tip

Tip...

Corporate trainers report that a higher share of students in e-based courses pass certification exams than those in instructor-led classes. Self-paced learning seems to improve retention rates.

Bright Idea

To get anywhere, IT professionals need both a college degree and a string of certifications in no particular order. Some students hop back and forth between college and training courses—often while already on the job. Why not be a one-stop shop that offers both types of education online to busy IT workers? If that's too big a task, then serve as a middleman for college courses, helping to land the student in the best online university for his or her needs while providing the IT coursework yourself. This way, you're not taking on the role of teaching both college and IT courses, but you are making some profit from both sides.

renew your status online and pay a couple hundred dollar annual fee every October. Depending on the program, you must deliver a certain number of courses during a one-year period to be allowed to renew your MCT status. Microsoft audits a certain percentage of trainers every year to make sure they are doing the job. In return, Microsoft grants you the necessary license; access to content, information, and marketing materials; and use of Microsoft brand identifications. Then, Microsoft refers students to you. Depending on your business, that could be 90 percent of your whole marketing program.

> Tip...
>
> **Smart Tip**
>
> What's the IT certification competition like? Find out quickly at Find Computer Schools (www.find-computer-schools.com), an IT web portal with a powerful database of IT certification training resources searchable by training type, topic, certification type, state, zip code, and numerous other parameters.

Certification always involves testing. The product vendor typically creates the tests. However, Microsoft solicits input from certain high-level training organizations. Also, if the topic is relatively new or you are unusually successful, you may be able to consult with vendors and influence the training criteria. You can also create your own tests! Among the 400 certifications offered by online test center giant Brainbench are generalized topics of its own creation that go way outside IT topics—for example, there are $50 tests on Advertising Industry Knowledge or Pharmaceutical Industry Knowledge.

Dauntless DANTES

Like all government agencies, the Department of Defense runs various programs to help underwrite the cost of independent training for armed forces personnel. Security is an obvious priority for all branches of the military nowadays. One such program is specifically designed to certify security professionals and goes by the acronym DANTES (Defense Activity for Non-Traditional Education Support). The mission of DANTES is to support the off-duty, voluntary education programs of the Department of Defense and to conduct special projects and development activities in support of education-related functions of the Department.

The program reimburses members of the Army Reserve, Army National Guard, and the Air Force Reserve for information security training courses. It acquaints them with private-sector security training practices. The U.S. Department of Veterans Affairs has similar reimbursements for other members of the military.

Brainbench has acquired such credibility that, after just four years in the industry, it can afford to offer certification exams independent of the direction of product vendors. At Brainbench, a MCSE exam is, instead, a Windows Administrator exam.

"Our tests are built purely from the application point of view without vendor biases," says Brainbench co-founder Mike Littman. "We're at a more granular level, where we're really focusing on real-world issues, as opposed to focusing too much on the products themselves."

Don't overlook professional development and managerial courses for IT pros. If they hope for advancement, they face the same personnel, scheduling, project management, and other managerial requirements that any MBA student faces.

This audience is already highly educated and quite open to suitable asynchronous learning. According to surveys by *Certification* magazine, about 65 percent of IT professionals looking for certification have earned a college degree, and 18 percent have a graduate or professional degree. The 35 percent who are not college graduates have taken classes at technical colleges and institutes.

Resume Builders

Here are just a few examples of the numerous certificates offered by online education businesses in conjunction with the major hardware and software manufacturers.

Cisco

Cisco Certified Network Associate (CCNA). Installs, configures, and operates routed LAN and WAN, as well as switched LAN networks. A brief example of what might be included in such a curriculum is:

- Building a simple Ethernet network
- Expanding the network
- Connecting networks
- Constructing network addresses
- Connecting remote networks
- Operating and configuring Cisco IOS switches and IOS routers
- Managing a network environment
- Administering network devices
- Routing Cisco networks
- Managing IP traffic on Cisco networks
- Expanding a Cisco network to a WAN

Resume Builders, continued

- Interconnecting Cisco networking devices
- Cisco networking technologies

Cisco Certified Network Professional (CCNP). Certification in installing, configuring, operating, and troubleshooting complex Cisco networks

Cisco Certified Network Design Professional (CCDP). A certificate in designing complex Cisco networks

Microsoft

Microsoft Certified Professional (MCP). Allows you to utilize your skills in a particular Microsoft product.

Microsoft Certified Desktop Support Technician (MCDST). For troubleshooting Microsoft Windows on desktops.

Microsoft Certified Application Developer (MCAD). For developing and maintaining applications and components

Microsoft Certified Professional Developer (MCPD). For those looking to serve as experts in Windows development, web application development, or enterprise applications development.

Novell

Certified Novell Administrator (CNA). The first step toward the CNE, this certificate is for IT professionals working on the administration of Novell networking systems and providing support to users.

Certified Novell Engineer (CNE). Advanced Novell Certificate

Novell Certified Linux Engineer (CLE). For mastery of advanced SUSE Linux Enterprise Server administration.

Oracle offers an OCA, OCP, and certificates for its Siebel Products, and Sun Microsystems has Java certifications. In short, all of the software manufacturers provide some type of product specific certificates. Places like the Computing Technology Industry Association (CompTIA) also offer a variety of more broad-based, vendor-neutral, general certificates in convergence and troubleshooting for integrated systems and security.

These are among the many online IT certificates that you can provide in conjunction with the vast software environment. Keep in mind, however, that there is a lot of competition, so you need to stay on top of the ever-changing technology needs of business—possibly focusing on one specific industry.

6

Lifelong Online Learning

Most of the learning you do in your life has nothing to do with a degree or a certification. It has to do with interests. Online education is carving out an ever-larger role in this personal learning—whether it's a CD-ROM that polishes French conversational skills or an interactive quiz on a parenting education site.

Personal learning is the broadest of the online learning markets, but the hardest to define. Many promising and prominent ventures have flopped, for example, the edutainment software companies that melted away during the past decade. Fathom, the internet academic consortium, quietly folded its tent in 2003. And then there was the Global Education Network, which was backed by a major financial institution, but mistakenly hired a very young MTV generation CEO and soon disappeared.

It is, therefore, essential to get a grasp of the broader potential demographic market, which is 15 to 66 and beyond. Not everyone is immersed in the latest technology nor is everyone looking for "sound byte bits of learning." For example, the attention span of someone interested in English lit. or political science is typically greater than the average reality TV or MTV aficionado. The learning curve on how to reach the broader market is still being built.

Over time, online education is likely to become more deeply embedded in our culture, just as computers, cell phones, and other information and communication appliances have become part of life in the 21st century for all age groups. Diligent entrepreneurs like you will make this happen. In this chapter, we sketch some more of the online learning opportunities, starting with the various demands of customers in different age groups. Some aspects of this market, such as the potential interest among seniors, may surprise you.

Kids Are Born to It

They say if you want to learn something, learn it while you're young. Technology has proven that adage to be true. Just ask a 9-year-old to program your cell phone. He or she will do it in minutes. The new technology is second nature to our children. They were born into TV households; many had a remote control in their hands by the time they could walk. Now, they are growing up with computers.

Today's kids are not just familiar with computers; a large majority have their own computers, cell phones, and iPods from the age of 8. Laptop computers are largely found among high school and college students, many of whom use them to upload online educational materials or do research for school from a variety of locations because wireless capabilities

> Tip...
>
> **Smart Tip**
>
> Think niches—and sometimes even niches within niches. Take financial skills, for example: Different versions of the Investing for Success online interactive workshops have been developed by the Investment Company Institute. One was developed with the Coalition of Black Investors Investment Education Fund. A bilingual one was created with the Hispanic College Fund.

have expanded rapidly. It's also entirely possible today to fuse learning into the cell phone via text messages—although most students are not yet very receptive, considering their cell phones for personal matters and not for school. Even iPods have learning potential. For example, some kids have uploaded their Bar Mitzvah lessons in between rock and pop selections. As new communication applications emerge, the clever entrepreneur will think ahead and be ready to embrace new forms of electronic learning without sacrificing content or integrity.

So what are the opportunities for online education in the kids' market? While it may seem that kids are born with Nintendo controllers in their hands, they actually have a long learning curve for mastering computers. Typically this is done with a little adult guidance and a lot of trial and error. Simple online learning "courses" and help systems can lend a hand.

There are literally thousands of web sites for children and teens, from early childhood learning up through high school. Sites such as FunBrain.com, Discovery.com, ScienceMaster.com, Americaslibrary.gov, Powertolearn.com, and Scholastic.com are designed to teach kids while trying to make the process fun and graphically exciting. Plenty of other sites, such as kidssites.com, serve as portals, or review sites, linking to the many online educational possibilities available. Additionally, for nearly a decade now, children have also benefited from well-crafted educational programs on CD-ROM, such as The Learning Company's Carmen Sandiego, Reader Rabbit, and Zoombinis series. Note that creating such packages, marketing them, and finding distribution for them is extremely expensive. Many web sites offer similar but abbreviated content, typically free material that supports other products. In both cases, your entry point may be to provide contract services to those creating the content.

Teens Drive the Market

They may not be interested in what you—or their parents—want to promote, but teens are very definitely tuned in to the internet and technology in general. In fact, when it comes to any technology purchase for the family, teens rule. "Parents may control the checkbook, but teens wield the most influence in technology purchasing decisions in American households because they have the most interest," explains research firm InsightExpress. Teens cast the deciding vote a majority of the time in the purchase of everything from MP3 players and internet access to cell phones, digital cameras, and even laptops and notebook computers.

CD-ROMs for learning languages also have proved reasonably popular (and effective). To effectively start a children's educational web site, you need to

1. understand the specific educational needs of each, or any one, grade level,
2. have input from teachers and learning specialists,
3. create a dynamic presentation on your web site (without overdoing the bells and whistles), and
4. make learning fun.

Because there is so much free content available, you will need to support such a site through advertising, educational grants, sponsorship, and/or selling products (which can be anything from books to DVDs and CDs to calculators).

Most significantly, look for places where you can fill a void and present material in a new manner that stimulates learning activity. Do plenty of market research and know your young demographic audience. This means everything from interviewing teachers and learning specialists to surfing a couple hundred web sites for kids and determining what you do and do not like—while looking for voids to fill. Remember, you need not recreate the wheel, you simply need to find a new way of effectively selling and marketing it.

Adult Fare

We discussed college-age adults in Chapter 4. As people move on to full-time work and/or raising a family, their educational needs and desires may change dramatically. But their quest for learning continues, and it's not all about work and credentials either.

One example is learning about software. You'd be surprised at how many people are regularly frustrated with everyday software programs and how few really get the most from these tools. Many are interested in learning more for personal as well as business use. This market stays fresh because these applications change often and are so complicated and feature-rich. It really takes a lot to learn how to take full advantage of them, and courses getting the most out of the latest software can be big business. The same holds true for other aspects of technology, such as a course on getting the most out of your digital camera.

There's also a wide sweep of noncredit, instructor-led continuing education courses offered by community colleges and other traditional education providers, as well as a growing number of online entrepreneurs like you. You can learn about Renaissance painting, the history of Iraq, the proper way to write a movie script, or any of hundreds of other subjects. There is a nationwide pool of potential customers—if you can find compelling ways to create and market these offerings. Some may be suitable, naturally, for self-study courses offered on CD-ROM or the Net. (Your best strategy may be to create the instructor-led course, and then if interest seems high enough, repackage the material in product form.)

There aren't three or four continuing education markets; there are three or four thousand, depending on how you target and serve specific audiences. Some are less obvious—such as the senior, which we'll look at next.

Bright Idea

If you're not sure where to find course ideas for adult learners, check out the evening course listing at nearby colleges or browse established brick-and-mortar learning center brochures from places like the Learning Annex in cities such as New York, Los Angeles, Chicago, Boston, and Toronto. You should also check out the talk shows to see what guests are talking about. Often authors and experts are soon-to-be teachers in such adult learning environments. Keep your eyes and ears open at all times to the needs, wants, and interests of the 29- to 69-year-old demographic audiences.

Seniors Go PC

Baby boomers are getting long in the tooth. The leading edge of the generation is reaching retirement age, swelling the numbers of what already was a fast-growing population of older Americans. People are living longer as a result of better medical practices, new drugs, and healthier lifestyles. The 2000 U.S. Census found that about 12 percent of the U.S. population (35 million people) were aged 65 or older, a number that is expected to double to 70 million by the year 2030.

Increasingly, however, this population is still on the job. A recent survey of workers aged 45 and older by the American Association of Retired Persons (AARP) showed that 80 percent expect to work past 65. Whether they retire, seniors can tap computers to open up a new world of information and communications. Computers can manage finances, expand their minds, and help them stay productive and active after retirement, an important component in living a longer, healthier, happier life.

It's true that this is easily the least computer-literate group in our society. Because this generation did not grow up with computers or use them early on in their careers, many have become more comfortable using other means of accessing and/or storing information. The idea of learning the computer is met by resistance by a large segment of this population. However, once the door is opened, thousands of seniors have found the computer to be a marvelous way of learning, maintaining current interests, and keeping abreast of the latest news. Places like SeniorNet.com and AARP's web site are ideal starting points for learning more about using the computers and finding online learning opportunities.

"It's very typical for seniors to declare that they are just not good with computers," report Devin Williams and Sarah Chapman, who formed Spry Learning Co. in Portland, Oregon, to bring computer literacy and online learning to retirees. Spry has devised dozens of classes on everything from computer basics to managing stock portfolios that have brought thousands of seniors into the computer age.

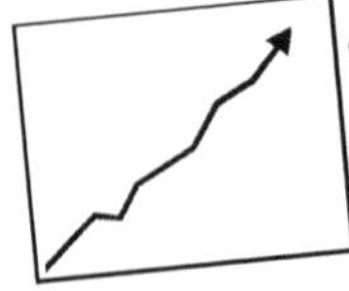

Stat Fact

Once properly introduced, 69 percent of wired seniors are on the internet every day, compared with 56 percent of other wired Americans, according to the Pew Internet & American Life Project survey.

Williams and Chapman note that seniors have wide variations in interests and capabilities. They have found distinct differences in the manual dexterity, vision, attention span, and mental acuity of younger seniors compared with those over 70 or so. These different physical skills and learning styles require different teaching styles. But it's worth the effort.

Chapman and Williams report that they found very little PC use among the 46,000 senior communities that are Spry's targeted niche. The two co-founders spent a year working in senior communities before launching Spry, doing onsite research and designing their products, which ultimately turned out to be a body of coursework and teaching methods delivered in different ways. Some courses are taught over the Net, but most are taught by the recreational and nursing staff in senior communities.

"Once seniors have overcome their fear of computers, they become very enthusiastic users," report Chapman and Williams. Searching health-related web sites for detailed information is very popular. E-mail helps with socialization because seniors aren't as isolated from distant family and friends. Additionally, chat rooms promote dialogue. Computers can also offer recreation and entertainment, particularly for

Health Benefit

Computers can do seniors a world of good. A study by scientists at the Rush Alzheimer's Disease Center of Chicago's Rush-Presbyterian-St. Luke's Medical Center found that more frequent participation in mentally stimulating activities is associated with a reduced risk of Alzheimer's disease (AD). The study found that, depending on the amount of increase in cognitive activities, seniors can reduce the risk of developing AD by 33 to 47 percent.

seniors who aren't very mobile. The machines also promote independence; people are able to carry out business activities such as shopping or personal banking from home.

Using a computer can be a physical challenge, yet it also can enhance fine motor skills and hand-eye coordination for individuals who struggle in those areas. Alternatively, accessories such as a touch pad, trackball, or voice-control system can make a computer easier to use.

Tip...

Smart Tip

The socialization aspects of education are particularly important to seniors. For many, it's not just education; it's recreation. Both personal contact and fun loom large in senior choices for

Learning new skills gives seniors a sense of accomplishment that spurs them on. The mental and physical activity of computing has been shown to sharpen the mental acuity of seniors and promote good health overall. "But you have to take it slow and take nothing for granted," says Williams. You have to create coursework or lesson plans that are incredibly literal and take things step-by-step.

Continuing Education Reborn

The community outreach program of MiraCosta College in San Diego County is a good example of the varied approaches educational institutions are taking to personal online education. It also highlights the possibilities for entrepreneurial involvement as circumstances and student needs dictate. MiraCosta offers local community members a variety of computer and computer-assisted courses in the traditional classroom setting at its campuses. Most of these are conducted in partnership with local entrepreneurs.

No topic is inappropriate for online education. Some can be distinctly avante garde. For example, MiraCosta has offered a class titled "Trade Worldwide in Nine Weeks." The course in building your own import/export business is delivered during two-hour synchronous lecture and discussion segments. All software and materials are downloaded on the Net. The instructor is a local e-learning entrepreneur working under the aegis of the college. He gains credibility from the association as well as benefiting from marketing through the college catalog and the ads MiraCosta runs in local newspapers. He shares revenues from the classes with the college. MiraCosta's business development director, Leon Levy, calls his

Stat Fact

The majority of colleges (close to 90 percent) report that they operate a distance learning program, with nearly half of these schools offering accredited degrees over the internet, according to market research.

Meeting an Existing Need

A very unique and highly unprecedented online education story comes from the formation and accreditation of Western Governors University. At a meeting of the Western Governors Association in Park City, Utah, the subject of education was raised. It was not the reason the meeting was convened, nor was it a scheduled discussion. However, once a discussion of higher education arose, the governors of several states all voiced a similar concern about spiraling costs, lack of skilled graduates entering the workforce in their states, and new technologies not being introduced fast enough to their states' systems of higher education, many of which were unresponsive to the new technology or unwilling to change.

This shared concern of 19 governors prompted the idea for Western Governors University. Each governor contributed $100,000 from his state. From that point forward, the university would be private and not-for-profit, offering online competency-based programs only in areas with a need for skilled graduates.

In time an interregional accrediting committee was created and WGU gained accreditation. Today, Western Governors University is regionally accredited by the Northwest Commission on Colleges and Universities, one of the major accrediting commissions recognized by the U.S. Department of Education and the Council for Higher Education Accreditation. Programs and degrees are offered for teaching, business, health, and information technology.

school's approach pretty typical of similar institutions around the country—that is, using a blend of online learning and traditional education modes as the situation demands.

7

Course Planning and Offerings

This is an opportune time to discuss some of the general needs of an online education business. No matter how your technological infrastructure is built, the computer techies as well as the lifelong learners need a clear picture of what you are offering and how it is presented. Therefore, you need to map out your presentation on your web site and how you present your online courses.

Your Course Catalog or List of Participating Schools

Whether you are presenting original course content or serving as a middleman and linking to courses from Devry, Kaplan, Walden, and other leading online institutions, your course directory needs to be well-organized and carefully written to provide a succinct summary of what the course offers. Offerings can be categorized in a number of ways with easy search options—by program of interest, degree, accreditation, certificate, type of course (i.e., seminar), and so on. For example, Degrees.com lets you search for a course at one of several schools by level of degree, subject category, or even most popular courses.

The key is to make it as simple as possible to find a course or program by outlining the requirements, credits received per course, and accreditation available for completing the program. As in e-commerce, you want landing pages for customers to learn more about the course, the program, and/or the college or university. As you design pages for other universitys' programs, you want to maintain consistency, while still including all the necessary data. You can also design sites for partnerships with other businesses that match well with your demographics. For example, eLearners.com has a site page for its partnership with Sallie Mae. Primarily known for real estate loans, Sallie Mae also provides an answers.com web site designed to help deal with financial issues for students with loans. This ties in nicely with the eLearners market.

If you are providing original content, then you will set up your own landing pages, where students learn more about a course or program of study before making a commitment. The landing page is often overlooked by new entrepreneurs, but a staple of more experienced e-retailers, such as Amazon, where you'll click on a book for a detailed page about the book. The idea is to avoid leapfrogging the consumer from a blurb about a course to a registration form or "shopping cart." People need a moment to make an informed decision before simply buying. You also want to include some information here on your instructor.

Your actual online catalog should be comprehensive but not overwhelming to the eye. If you are offering degrees or certification, you'll need a link from your home page and from your course catalog to some basic information on what each degree indicates and what is required to complete a degree program. If, for example, you explain what a Master's degree is, you should then follow it with a description of the various types of Master's degrees, such as MA, MS, etc. and what is required for each.

Walk Yourself Through

Before you start designing your online learning web site, take a mental tour of what you need and list it. Then, perhaps, view some of your competitors and see how they have mapped it all out. Some sites jump immediately to a page asking the user to fill out information. While this works for Phoenix Online University, which is well established, it may not be the best approach for a new business. Remember, you are selling, so you will need to put your products upfront—subjects, schools, or programs offered—a link to your course listings, an "about us" page, a link to information about registration, perhaps a FAQ page, maybe a link to an online educational advisor, and perhaps to articles and content about online learning. In short, you need to think about all the things you would want to see if you were about to take an online course or go for your degree online.

Hot Topics and Unique Courses

Team Building, Early Childhood Development, Web Design, Graphic Design, Yoga, Aromatherapy, Memoir Writing, and on it goes. The list of possible topics and courses is endless. Your mission when formulating courses to create and/or courses to market is to find the areas of the greatest interest. This means doing plenty of homework well before school even begins. Consider the articles you read and the topics on news magazine television programs. Sexual harassment, guarding against identity theft, parenting drug- and alcohol-free teenagers, creating an efficient home office environment, and Middle East tension and conflicts are just a few among many topics that are drawing significant attention. Can you offer courses that offer solutions, discussion, or even a debate on what is in the news? Many current events tie into history. You can present a new approach to teaching history by linking its significance to current events. Think about what courses will educate people and/or provide them with information that they can use at work or personally.

Reviewing the courses offered by the many leading online education providers gives you, like other good entrepreneurs, an opportunity to seek a competitive edge. Find something that is not being offered and offer it. Of course, this is not that easy with the vast course selections available. Therefore, you may need to find new ways to present familiar subject matter or find experts in the field who can offer a unique perspective on a familiar topic.

Dollar Stretcher

Package similar courses together. For students who are not following a course of study for a specific degree, you can entice them to take a second course, for less money perhaps, by linking similar subjects.

Additionally, if you can add interesting peripheral materials, your courses can stand out from the competition. For example, perhaps your course on McCarthyism includes a video of Arthur Miller's play *The Crucible*, to be viewed and discussed in conjunction with the period it was written, the early 1950s, and how the witch hunts (from the 17th century) were as relevant to the 1950s as they are today.

The Online Teaching Modality

Unlike traditional classroom learning, which is teacher focused, online courses are typically student focused and driven by the efforts of the students to respond to the curriculum. This can be effective if the curriculum is designed for independent research and study, and the students are prepared. The role of the instructor is less communicator and more learning guide, selecting appropriate content, asking thought-provoking questions, and opening up a forum for discussion. The instructor is then able to facilitate and monitor the work of the students through deadlines for projects as well as tests, discussion groups, chat rooms, and e-mails. Because online learning is still new to many instructors, you may need to provide training in how to motivate students through the internet and how to present course matter that is informative and translates well over the medium.

A criticism of online education is that it leaves too much in the hands of the student to comprehend the information and this can jeopardize the quality of the education because the student is only responsible for what he or she puts into and takes away from the course. It is also harder to hold a student responsible via the internet.

Arguments in favor of online education stress that the student in a traditional class setting may only be walking away with that which

Smart Tip

Tip...

Traditional classrooms are social: students talk to one another, share ideas, and exchange information. Your online classes also should be social. Provide your students with access to online forums, chat rooms, and message boards to give them an opportunity to meet one another.

he or she learns from instructor's take on a subject. By opening up the field to a much wider range of resources, the student can interpret a wider range of viewpoints on a given topic. Online education also helps to level the playing field by providing a more nondiscriminatory student-teacher environment. Of course, responsibility in any learning situation still falls on the shoulders of the student to do his or her own work.

This new teaching modality requires instructors to prepare a course as both a teacher and an online designer. While he or she should not be in the position of handling the technical aspects of posting the data, it is the role of a good instructor to determine how to mix the tools of online communication most effectively to create a well-balanced learning experience. This includes the instructor's expertise along with the various other perspectives. The best online instructors have mastered and taken advantage of the potential for blending their own expertise with the many resources available to their students.

Staying in Synch—or Not

Synchronous courses can offer more familiar kinds of instructor-student interactions, which offer great appeal. But they also bring many other issues. You can sell a canned course to as many students as you want, but you can't have an interactive, real-time online seminar with 1,000 students participating at the same time without a huge investment in back-end infrastructure. For the experience to be truly taking place in real time, the instructor must be broadcasting by video and the students must be equipped to receive it, which requires a broadband connection, a decent PC, and sometimes special software. There must be a set time and place, which limits the flexibility in time schedules. Also, course size must be somewhat limited if there is an opportunity for feedback. However, in the right environment, this type of learning can bring a real-life class environment together with students spread out over the country or the world.

Students and teachers often prefer asynchronous online learning because of the freedom it brings by allowing everyone to work at their own convenience. Compared to driving across town or going on a week-long training mission, being available for a few hours a week doesn't seem like asking much. But if it's 2 P.M. Wednesday and your boss just asked you to take care of an emergency, will you really tell him "Sorry, it's time for my class?" On the other hand, the problem for many people is too much flexibility in how and when they get the work done. This prompts students to procrastinate and then cram the work in at the deadline, managing to meet the requirements while actually learning very little. Therefore, it is important to motivate your students and to set fairly strict deadlines.

Mixing the Best Blend

Whatever subjects and curriculum you choose, you will still need to deliver coursework that improves upon seminars presented by traditional providers. People need incentives for adopting new ways of doing things—the lack-of-travel incentive notwithstanding.

One way to add value is to blend synchronous and asynchronous coursework with class time. Students can study presentations and take tests online (which can be easily updated or otherwise customized), augmenting classroom work. That's how the business education programs work at MiraCosta Community College (www.miracosta.edu) in Oceanside, California. Leon Levy, director of business development, reports enthusiastic acceptance among local firms.

Making It Sing

To succeed, online education initiatives must more than just deliver educational materials. They must become a more strategic component of the overall business environment. The modern customer, online student, is seeking more than just a simplistic text-based course. To be successful, make sure you've covered these three bases:

1. *Add interactivity.* Plain text-based training material may be useful, but it's limited. No one likes to read at length on a computer. Students won't retain as much; they'll get bored. Corporate students, as well as many home users today, are well-equipped, so add interactive elements such as simulation, collaboration, appropriate graphics, and online testing. If you don't add value above the "old ways," you're reducing your competitiveness and limiting your profit potential.
2. *Blend learning styles and keep it personal.* You'll want to highlight personal interaction with bulletin boards, e-mail, scheduled web chats, and possibly videoconferencing. Use the tools of technology to encourage student interaction.
3. *Stay current.* Yes, there are evergreen courses that will last forever, but you need to stay on top of what the market demands. New software means updating your course listings. New ways of conducting business transactions? New popular cultural trends? Whatever you are selling, make sure you remain current—even if it means new presentations of tried and true subject matter.

Workers can take classes on campus or learn asynchronously at their own pace through the college's web site, but MiraCosta's Business Development program also brings classes to the workplace. In addition to the usual computer basics and software training courses, classes are offered to improve workplace skills—English as a Second Language, Workplace Math, and Business Communications. The classes blend computer use and classroom experience as appropriate. Called "blended learning," or the "hybrid method" (a popular term these days), the mix of classroom and online coursework allow students to connect with instructors and other students, while not having to deal with regular travel time to complete the coursework, which can be finished online.

While such hybrid learning essentially eliminates the long-distance aspect of taking courses far from home, it does provide instructors with a way of mixing seminars with other forms of interactive, often visual, learning mediums that can be found online. A wealth of interesting content can be at the fingertips of the students on the internet that is not available in a standard classroom setting.

The method is still fairly new, but reports have been very positive in the early going, with instructors reporting very good rates of success. By actually having some face-to-face interaction, students are typically more self-motivated because there is a greater sense of accountability than is typically found in a strictly online course. Additionally, the active role by the student in her own learning gives her greater involvement (or ownership) in the course material than would be true sitting in a lecture hall taking notes. For the best results, testing can once again bring the students together in a traditional setting to insure the integrity of the student performance.

Both the University of Phoenix and Devry University offer the combined classroom/online hybrid learning programs. "In our Ph.D. program, the learners are required to attend a true residential session once a period," says Stephen Shank of Capella University (www.capellauniversity.edu) in Minneapolis. "We actually rent a college campus to do that. In addition, those same learners attend two seminars a year, which are held in hotel conference spaces around the country." Everything else is online. Spohn Training (www.spohntraining.com) in Austin, Texas, also exemplifies the blended approach, combining both classroom and online learning effectively in interactive synchronous classes.

Corporations very often find that a combination of classroom work and online instruction can provide the most effective approach to employee training. Online education can be very effective in this market when blended with traditional classes.

The World of Online Instructors

What's a course without an instructor? While computer-based learning does exist, there is still a bias toward instructor-based courses in most fields. Online education has brought with it the need for online instructors from a wide variety of backgrounds and disciplines. As online education grows, more and more professionals are moving into teaching positions, enjoying the ability to teach from a homebase or from their own office without having a daily commute to a campus. Many professionals are moonlighting. Because one of the criticisms of online education is that anybody can bill themselves as a teacher and throw a course online, you need to provide background information about your instructors. Of course, before doing so, you need to make sure that whomever you interview for an online teaching position is who he says he is. Background checks are as essential as they are when hiring employees in any business. This is true of teachers you meet in person as well as instructors teaching one of your courses from another continent. Credibility, or lack thereof, can make or break you.

Online teachers typically have both credentials (masters degrees or at least high-level certificates in their fields) and several years of experience in the field. The other qualifications include a comfort level with online communications tools, sufficient time available to formulate a lesson plan, and strong communication skills—writing is key because the written word is the primary means of communication on the internet.

The online education instructor's role changes, especially in asynchronous courses, but he is still a central figure. The instructor must update course content, run online forums, answer questions from students promptly via e-mail or chats, grade papers, and assume other typical teaching duties. In addition, he must stay well versed in what is offered as reference materials on (and off) the internet. After all, an instructor expects his students to utilize the medium to the fullest and seek answers to complex or controversial questions; he needs to know where those students look for the answers.

Finding Instructors

You must pay instructors on an ongoing basis. You may also have to provide them with computer hardware, software, and other resources. And—the most difficult part—you have to find them and keep them.

The traditional academic model uses instructors with Ph.D.s. It's not unusual for someone to spend years earning a Bachelor's degree, then a Master's degree, and a Ph.D., and then accept a teaching position, never leaving academia. More business-oriented learning organizations, like the University of Phoenix Online, tend to take their instructors from the real world. Their theory is that it's better to learn about business administration from somebody who has run a company than from somebody who has an MBA but has never left the ivory tower.

Today, you'll find instructors by looking for people who have had an impact in their fields and know how to clearly communicate what they have accomplished to others. There are many people who have done well in their fields but are unable to

Bright Idea

Along with student enrollment and payment guidelines, write out guidelines for instructors. Just because employees, instructors in this case, are not working on site does not mean that set rules of conduct, procedures, and guidelines do not apply. Instructors need to take this business seriously and understand that failure to maintain their course schedule or acting in any inappropriate manner will not be tolerated.

clearly communicate or articulate their success. Conversely, there are those who talk up a good game and have plenty to say, but have not had the experience and success from which others can really benefit. You want instructors with experience and expertise in their field and some communication skills.

In time, with good marketing and a positive reputation, instructors may be seeking you out. When CourseBridge began, founder Linda Casselman had just received her Teacher/Trainer of Adults certificate and was looking for work, so she started out teaching online elsewhere. "I quickly became dissatisfied with the way that business was operating and so decided to start my own. Since my partner is a programmer-analyst, he built the site and set everything up so it cost very little, except time, to get started," explains Linda. However, once CourseBridge launched and marketed, they encouraged instructors to find them. "We don't go looking for instructors; they find us," says Linda, who has an online application form at the web site that potential instructors can use to apply to teach at CourseBridge.

"If their course is something suitable for us, I check out their experience with the topic, as well as their teaching experience, and then request their course. After reviewing it and checking that it is indeed a properly designed course, I know if they are qualified to offer it through us or not," explains Linda, of the CourseBridge way of finding instructors. "CourseBridge was primarily created as a place where I could offer my own courses," notes Linda of her entrepreneurial start in the business. "We were interested in offering writing-related courses as that's what sells best. I do, however, consider other courses if I feel they fit in," she adds.

You can also have instructors pitch you courses. However, let it be known the type of courses and the teaching modality you are looking for. Have some general information on your web site for new instructors about whether you are offering asynchronous, synchronous, mixed online, or traditional courses, and what responsibilities teachers have (in general) to your business and to the students. Set up a framework by which potential instructors can propose their offerings. Then determine if they meet your needs academically, technologically, and from an overall marketing perspective. Does the course speak to your target audience?

From a practical perspective, you might also try advertising for instructors on any number of job boards such as Monster (www.monster.com), looking for individuals with teaching backgrounds. Also keep an eye out for "job wanted" classifieds in online learning newsletters such as the Virtual University Gazette (www.geteducated.com). Generally, you'll want to build a stable of highly reliable freelancers, reducing your administrative and tax payment hassles, and your HR expenses. As you start making contacts, your instructors may know of others they can refer to help you build your instructor base.

Training and Setting Parameters

Most online universities offer training for their teachers in how to utilize their specific structure to teach online. As an entrepreneur, it is very important that your teachers understand both the technology and the methodology of your learning institution. Remember, the reputation and credibility of your business is on the line every time an instructor embarks on a new course. Therefore, you need to establish policies and parameters prior to bringing in instructors. Parameters are particularly important regarding e-mail, IM, and chat communications, where a casual atmosphere can occasionally ellicit unprofessional comments or tangential conversations. Experience and credentials are not enough when hiring instructors. You need professionals who can handle the course materials as well as student-instructor interactions appropriately.

Additionally, organizational and scheduling skills are even more important for an online instructor than for a professor in a traditional setting. For example, in a traditional university each instructor sets up her office hours. Then if she is not in her office or the door is closed and locked, students simply cannot meet with that instructor. Online, however, student meetings and communication can take place around the clock. The virtual office has no door. Therefore, parameters need to be set up very carefully. Instructors will reply in 12 hours, 24 hours, between 2 P.M. and 4 P.M. every day, or whatever works for your school and your instructors.

The concept of student participation also changes dramatically in the online setting, where a student cannot simply raise her hand. Discussion boards and chat rooms are one answer to that problem, but motivating students to get involved and take advantage of such opportunities is another issue entirely. Therefore, it is typically recommended that instructors make some type of participation mandatory for passing a course. Perhaps a student needs to participate in three of seven available chat room hours per week, thus maintaining the benefit of a flexible online schedule while also forging some connection with the student in a real time environment.

Of course, there are students that thrive on participation and excel in areas that invite a variety of opinions, discussion, and even debate. It is here where the instructor needs to present additional challenges and set up ways and means by which these students can participate in a more meaningful manner, perhaps by forging a new, more indepth, discussion group. Of course, there are students that are shy in any classroom setting, and you'll find these students participate more infrequently in online chats and on discussion boards. The instructor also needs to find ways in which to engage these students through some means of written communication.

Plusses and Minuses of Online Teaching

Plusses

- *Flex schedule.* Allows instructors greater flexibility in time and location of job activities; this also makes it easier for working professionals to teach courses.
- *Pull from numerous sources.* Forget a few textbooks, the internet makes it possible to disseminate a greater range of materials than a traditional class, through multimedia platforms and a variety of new tools of online communication.
- *Interactive learning.* Provides for greater interactivity for your students; can become more vested in the course by such hands-on activities.

Minuses

- *Lots of technology.* A dedicated instructor must stay on top of the technology learning curve, which requires a good aptitude for computer tech materials, including graphics and multimedia software.
- *Computer problems.* Where there are computers, there are glitches. This may or may not be in your control, depending on whose computer is failing to send/receive the message. Troubleshooting is not the responsibility of the instructor. However, she is often caught in the middle of the problem and needs to be apprised of some helpful means of solving computer problems. Unfortunately the quality of the course will suffer if the technology cannot support the efforts of the instructor and the design of the course. Iron this out ahead of time.
- *Camaraderie.* Say what you will about a teachers' cafeteria, there is a sense of camaraderie found among teachers working together at any level that is lost in the isolation of online education. An exchange of teaching ideas, possible solutions to common problems, and other useful tidbits of information are exchanged when teachers work in close proximity. This does not mean that an instructor cannot communicate and, possibly, even meet with other online instructors. In fact, the dedicated instructor should make an effort to meet others in the field. This, however, takes additional effort in the online teaching community, and some instructors do not avail themselves of the opportunity to reach out and communicate with their peers.

Maintain Control

Running an online education business can be a akin to the juggler trying to keep several balls in the air at any given time. There's the business end, the technical side, and academic end, all of which need your constant attention. Even for the middleperson, selling courses offered by other teaching enterprises, there is still a need to oversee what is being taught, by whom, and from what institution. Don't shoot the messenger doesn't apply if you are the messenger offering substandard courses on your web site, even if they are at other schools.

It is up to you as an entrepreneur to continuously review course curriculum, the background and credibility of instructors, and the design of each course. Among the common problems you will run into are instructors who crave bells and whistles and instructors who are jacks of all trades, or so they say. The first group will want to utilize all of the high-tech possibilities to create an online extravaganza. It is up to you to remind this instructor of budget constraints and reel him in. In the second group are the instructors who have come onboard to teach a class or two or three. However, very often at the behest of the entrepreneur, the experienced accountant, seasoned writer, or long-time investment advisor ends up teaching five or six courses, often on topics where she has no particular expertise. It's very easy to call on the same expert every time you are looking to add another course on a topic. Likewise, it's very easy to say yes if the instructor asks to teach additional courses. Keep in mind, however, that the workload should not overwhelm the instructor. She will fall behind or burn out if too much is asked, and the courses will suffer. For that reason, many schools limit the number of courses an instructor can teach.

Protect Your Property

You may accumulate a great deal of intellectual property within your online learning company. Intellectual property is different from physical property or the medium over which it is delivered. You can't pick it up and feel it, but you can still own it. And it can't be reused without permission of the owner. This book, for example, is a piece of intellectual property. It is more than just the paper it is printed on. The real meat of what you bought is the information contained on these pages. Entrepreneur Media owns this information, and you can't reprint it without our permission.

By the same token, if you are offering original material, you must protect yourself against other people taking it. This applies whether you password-protect the information or not. Even if you place it openly on the web for anybody to see, it's still

Creating Educators

For training seniors in computer basics, Spry Learning in Portland, Oregon, uses the staff at their residential communities and trains them. Spry also develops its own content. At first, it employed gerontologists and instructional designers to develop courses. However, now that it has a template, Spry can use creative and detail-oriented clerical staff to develop courses.

yours. When the internet first started, it was largely an academic exercise and was not used for commerce. Users got the mistaken idea that whatever appeared on the internet was free for the taking. As a tool of academia, the internet does indeed make a wonderful venue for the free exchange of ideas. But that is only one purpose. It is also a tool of commerce, and everything is not free.

There may be times when you want someone else to use your material, and you won't want to charge them anything for it. For example, if someone writes a paper about online education and uses a sample clip from one of your classes as an example—and speaks highly of it—you'll probably want to allow that. However, course content is owned by someone—either you or the instructor—depending on how you word your contracts with instructors and how you create, or obtain, courses. If, for example, an instructor, who has been teaching for years at a brick-and-mortar university comes to you with a course and asks if he or she may teach it through your learning business, that instructor may own the rights to that course. You can, therefore, accept or reject the course. However, if you accept it, unless he or she signs over all rights to you, once that instructor retires or stops teaching the course for any reason, you cannot simply take the course and have someone else teach it without permission from the instructor who owns the intellectual rights. Of course, this does not mean you cannot have a course on the subject matter because no one can claim that they own the rights to teach the Civil War or integrated algebra.

Make sure you know who owns the rights to the courses you are offering. You can always

Bright Idea

Every month, go to a search engine such as Google to search the web for your intellectual property appearing on other web sites without your authorization. If you find cases, you can issue a cease and desist letter; the offending party must either meet your financial terms or stop using your material. Often a simple e-mail message will suffice.

require instructors to sign a contract that says, you own all rights to the course. However, some instructors won't want to work with you. Of course, if you are teaching courses for a leading software vendor, they will likely insist upon owning the rights so that other schools can also teach users about their products.

8

Solid Foundations for Virtual Firms

In this chapter, we cover some of the basics that will serve as the foundation for your new business, including your mission statement, business name, and all-important business plan. You'll also have a few other considerations, including how to structure your company, what accreditations you may need, and how to find a good attorney and accountant to help you with the start-up process.

Mission: Entirely Possible

Why are you going into business? What is it you propose to do? Who will be your customers? What unique value will you provide for them? These are just some of the questions to consider in writing your mission statement.

A *mission statement* is a paragraph that succinctly describes the purpose and goals of your business in such a way as to appeal to all the different audiences that your business intends to serve. Your mission statement will be included in your business plan, press releases, white papers, and other sales or marketing materials. It may be included on your web site under the "about us" section. It tells all those who would invest in you, partner with you, or buy from you what your business approach is all about. It is also a touchstone that can help all the members of your company stay focused on your goals and operating principles.

Your mission statement must grab potential customers and communicate the most important things about doing business with you in a few sentences. It must be easy to read and understand. It must spark instant recognition among the people you hope to reach, although not necessarily among the world at large. It must be specific enough to communicate your business purpose, and yet flexible enough to respond to what the market tells you.

Time and again, successful entrepreneurs find that they need to shift to a related audience or a different distribution methodology. For example, while he was creating the business plan for the training reseller MySoftwareHelper, Mark Carey envisioned doing most of his business with consumers from his web site with a minority of sales coming through corporate accounts. However, after two years in business, he has found those opportunities reversed—and drastically so.

Carey wants his mission statement to appeal to single-unit buyers as well as corporate, government, and educational institutions that might buy site licenses as a result of his sales calls. On MySoftwareHelper's web site, here's how the business was initially described:

> *MySoftwareHelper offers the 'best-of-breed' software training solutions from leading providers for all major software applications, professional IT certifications, and 'soft skills' in a wide variety of self-paced formats to meet individual or business needs—regardless of your budget.*

Note that this mission statement spells out "individual" as well as "business" needs, although individuals currently make up a minority of MySoftwareHelper sales. Note also that it specifically mentions the broad categories of courses—major software applications, professional IT certifications, and "soft skills," but doesn't mention the vendors from whom MySoftwareHelper gets the courses, which could change. Likewise, it doesn't mention specific content like Microsoft Excel or Microsoft MCSE Certification, which could later be overshadowed by newer courses.

Make Your Case to the Right Jury

Generally, a mission statement isn't meant to provide product or service specifics—it's too short. Rather, it lays out broad principles that guide the business—a commitment that should make people trust you and want to do business with you. Note the differences in the audience targeted by Spry Learning and what is being communicated in the mission statement:

> *Spry Learning is dedicated to enriching the lives of older adults through life-long learning. Leveraging technology and the internet, we seek to engage the minds and spirits of our students—keeping them healthy and connected to their families and the world. All programs are designed to benefit older adults, their residential communities and their families. Exemplary customer service is our only acceptable standard.*

Again, there's nothing about the specific courses or training methodologies, even though its training methodology happens to be a key advantage for Spry. Instead, Spry outlines broad lifestyle rewards that will accrue to its customers as a result of its services. At the same time, it is unusually specific about the audience, which may well be appropriate in this case. Experience has taught the co-owners of Spry that this particular audience needs to hear this level of focus and arm-around-the-shoulder commitment.

Although the MySoftwareHelper and Spry Learning mission statements are about online learning and both are well-directed at their target audiences, imagine if Spry tried to market to a corporate or even IT audience using that mission statement. MySoftwareHelper's mission statement probably wouldn't strike a responsive chord with seniors either.

Of course, these companies could easily change their mission statements on their web sites in a few minutes, and even their written materials in a short time. But it would take a long time to change the impression of their brand that both companies have worked so hard to build, and that might cause confusion among customers.

Here's one more mission statement example:

> *Our vision is to become the leading internet resource for continuing education, information, and communication, the essential tools our clients need to be successful in the business world.*

This is the mission statement for the online learning site RedVector.com, which provides training to people who want to get ahead in corporations and institutions. It's aimed at individuals rather than companies, as its rather noncorporate name suggests.

About Us

Your the mission statement can be on the web site as an independent page or on the "about us" page. However, you may want to provide additional information about the company on the "about us" page. Unlike brick-and-mortar businesses, you have the opportunity to provide background on your company and update it as often as necessary without the expense of reprinting a brochure or waiting for the next annual report.

Spry Learning, whose mission statement was included above, uses the following "about us" statement on its web site to include its beginning and the progress that it has made.

> *Promoting and facilitating life-long learning are the guiding principles behind Spry Learning Company programs. In 1999, co-founders Devin Williams and Sarah Chapman began developing computer-based learning curricula for seniors living in residence centers. Their intention was to provide structured activities that enrich daily life. They were struck by research that shows how activity and learning can stave off isolation and several illnesses that afflict the elderly. After one-and-a-half years of pilot programs and study, the refined SpryCat™ program became the company's first marketed service.*

The "about us" page is significant in the online marketplace. It provides the reader with a brief background of you and your company. However, it also lets you boast a little about your achievements and accomplishments. And finally, it should put some names and even faces behind an anonymous web site. Remember, anyone can post a web site today, even one that looks elaborate. Therefore, you want to differentiate yourself, your business, and your credibility from would-be players who don't have a full-fledged online learning business. There are also a lot of potential degree mills and even scammers on the internet. The more credible information you provide about yourself and your business, the more you can ease the concerns of an increasingly cynical online audience.

Name that Firm

Picking the right name is very important because it's the first impression you make. Unlike a mission statement or an "about us" page, which the reader needs to look for, a company name is your moniker, your means of presenting yourself to the public at large.

Your business name can communicate who you are, who you serve, and even something critical about your mission. It may be very literal or it may be very subtle. The key is to create a name that defines your business while being simple (catchy even) and easy to remember. The "Namingstorming Worksheet" on page 84 can help.

For example, RedVector.com doesn't sell to the same corporate and institutional employees MySoftwareHelper does. Rather, it's much more narrowly targeted to serve "professionals in the engineering, architectural, interior

Tip...

Smart Tip

What's the first question to ask if your brainstorming session yields a name or URL you want to use for your business? Is it already in use? There are lots of ways to find out, but any web search engine will let you know if the name is taken and give you a quick list of all the variations on your preferred name. Keep a list as you go to avoid duplication. Your search may even spark ideas for variations.

Truly Excellent e-Names

As important as it is for you to lasso a good company name, you also need a memorable web address. These two should not diverge very much from one another. The length and configuration of your URL, the name people type into their web browsers to get to your web page, can make all the difference in how many people go through the trouble of typing your company name—and, therefore, navigating to your site. Forget about URLs with lots of symbols and hyphens (even if they're part of your business name like "E*Trade") or complex sentences like www.creativestrategiesincorporated.com. People will forget them, misspell them, or just not want to do the typing, depending on how elaborate they are. For that reason, you'll want to register your own domain, as opposed to being a subset of some internet Service Provider's domain. Additionally, as a business, you lose a lot of credibility if you do not have your own web domain these days.

You'll register for at least one domain name with one of the registration agencies—a trivial process that involves an annual fee of less than $50 (unless, of course, you are bidding on someone else's name). If your company's name is "E-learning Central," and your URL is www.elearningcentral.com, it will be relatively easy for people to think of you and to get to your web site. You'll pop up in more search engines too. But sorry, E-learning Central is one of those simple and descriptive names that is already taken.

Namestorming Worksheet

Don't have the money to pay a creative agency to think up a name for your new online learning company? Your business name may come to you in a flash in the shower or while driving on the freeway—or you could "brainstorm" it.

1. Get creative yourself by writing down as many descriptive words as you can think of that relate to your business. Here are a few to start with: education, training, learning, skills, development. ____________________

   ____

   ____

2. Then, add other words that relate to your target audience, such as: professional, career, children, seniors, IT, college, management skills. ____

   ____

   ____

3. Still others may relate to the type of training you're planning on delivering: programming, web design, computer basics, networking, ______________

4. Go to an online or written thesaurus and add all the synonyms, homonyms, and, maybe, even antonyms for these words. ____________________

   ____

   ____

   ____

5. Check the phone book for some ideas. ______________________________

   ____

   ____

   ____

6. One way to narrow down the finalists is to write each word on a slip of paper, mix them all up, and put them together at random like Scrabble until you come up with a combination that appeals to you.

design, landscape architecture, building inspection, construction, and land surveying industries." This is a subset of the audience MySoftwareHelper targets—one sufficiently distinct that the two groups of customers probably overlap very little.

What does MySoftwareHelper connote compared to RedVector.com? The first sounds friendly and paternal. The second is MTV-like, assertive, and cutting-edge as befits the audience of young professionals RedVector. com targets. "Vector," of course, is an engineering term. "Red" is hot and flashy, like that portion of an automobile tachometer indicating limit-pushing speeds—perhaps, like the trajectory of your career.

Spry Learning also is a good name choice for its audience. It includes "learning," which immediately tells us that it's an educational company. "Spry," meaning agile or nimble, might apply to a lot of audiences, but it matches perfectly with an image of active seniors.

Creative agencies charge corporations millions of dollars and take months or years to come up with the right name. In many cases, these are almost-words, collections of sounds that may be part-English, part-French, part-scientific terminology. They often sound familiar, but don't have a literal meaning—at least, not at creation. What's a "Verizon"? What's a "Celica"? Large companies, spend tons on money utilizing the skills of advertising agency personnel to then market the unique name and build up a curiosity among the public until the name catches on and becomes associated with the business through the advertising and marketing campaigns. Start-up companies (and most small to mid-sized companies in general) do not have the money or the time to follow such an elaborate strategy. Instead, they need to have a name that clearly lets readers of print media, Yellow Page browsers (online or printed), and web surfers know what you do.

Because web learning is not localized, unless you are combining your online courses with traditional classroom learning, you do not need (or want) to narrow your potential audience to a particular region or community. However, you do want to narrow your demographic audience unless you truly believe you can reach everyone, which isn't easy, or likely.

Dollar Stretcher

You can get an idea whether your favorite name infringes upon someone else's trademarks at NameProtect (www.nameprotect.com). It provides a partial list of trademarks using a particular word in the United States, Canada, and on the web for free, or a comprehensive list in a report for a fee. NameProtect will also help you register a trademark for a fee.

Brand Exercises

Your business name is a key asset, and companies frequently sue other companies, successfully, over the use of words. That's true even for everyday words like "windows" that become part of a recognizable trademark or "apple," which was the name of the Beatles record company long before there were Apple computers (the two companies settled their dispute after many years). It's also true for slang or shorthand. For instance, even though the military has used the term "intel" as shorthand for intelligence for decades, you would be ill-advised to try to open, say, a private detective web site which contains the word "intel" in the address. A lawsuit is almost guaranteed. Of course, you might prevail in court, but only if you have sufficient funds to protect your right to use the word. Even if you do, that time and effort is better placed elsewhere.

Bright Idea

Prior to selecting a name, you may want to test market it among friends and relatives to get an idea of which names grab their attention. Because they probably know your business idea, you can ask them if they did not know what you were planning, would they get an idea of the type of business you were opening . . . and to whom it would appeal.

To avoid a lawsuit, your business name and product and service names must be entirely original, while sparking instant recognition. You want to be careful not to infringe upon anyone else's copyrights or trademarks. Therefore, you can do a trademark search through the United States Patent and Trademark Office (www.uspto.gov).

Tip...

Smart Tip

To stake out your cyberturf, you must register not only your domain name, but also stake a claim to common variations of that name. You may even want to register close misspellings of the name. The popular web search engine Google.com registered some variations on the spelling, so that if you type gogle.com, gooole.com, or googel.com, you will get google. However, they didn't buy all of the common misspellings, so if you type Goole or Goggle, you'll get completely different sites.

Lawyers and Tigers and Bears

As you pick your company name, product names, and web domain name, and as you decide the organizational structure of your company, you're probably going to need legal services. That doesn't have to be as scary and expensive as it sounds. It's not an open-ended commitment. Most of your legal bills should come as a result of issues that need to be decided before you open your doors. After that, you will need legal guidance, but hopefully not on a very frequent basis.

Whether you operate out of a home office or downtown digs, there are several critical issues you face, subtle legal twists and turns that are beyond the experience of the layman and don't necessarily lend themselves to common sense.

Dollar Stretcher

Don't necessarily hire the first lawyer you find—or the most expensive. Shop around, interviewing a few lawyers over the phone first and then in person. Don't be intimidated into paying hourly rates for those interviews. Also, don't hire a lawyer on a contingency basis. Insist on piecework and an estimate in advance for the cost of the specific services you need.

Unless you've been there before, you'll need a lawyer to explain the ins and outs of different methods of incorporation, copyrights, trademarks, logos, and common business contracts. This is not the time to hire your brother-in-law, the matrimonial attorney. It's the time to hire a qualified business attorney. A lawyer should check to make sure that your company and product names don't infringe upon anyone else's copyrights or trademarks. You may want to trademark your company name and logo. You may even have a process for which you want to apply for a patent. Web businesses also need a carefully crafted privacy statement.

In addition, you will have to define the rights of course content as discussed earlier. Who owns the rights? Rights issues can be very complicated, and an attorney can help you determine how to handle such issues. Make sure to address them. Likewise, if your courses utilize outside materials, such as photographs, written works, or perhaps a video tape, you need to have the rights to use such materials on your web site.

You'll want some legal help when putting together contracts with your instructors or with vendors. And, you will want to have an attorney review your web site before you launch.

The same holds true when selecting an accountant. Get some good referrals from people you trust and go with whomever you feel has a grasp of small business and the type of enterprise your are starting—not your neighbor's son who just graduated last week.

What Form Should Your Business Take?

One of the most important services a lawyer will provide is helping you settle on the type of legal entity your business should be. Very early on in the process of starting your new business, you will need to determine this. Will it be a sole proprietorship? A corporation? Limited liability company? Partnership? For this decision, you should definitely consult with your attorney as well as your accountant.

Many online learning businesses operate as sole proprietorships, often known as Schedule C businesses because of the forms they use when reporting their federal taxes. Other entrepreneurs elect instead to incorporate. Let's talk a little about these two business structures.

One of the advantages to forming a business as a sole proprietorship is that it's easy to do. Basically, the only work you're going to have to do is to obtain whatever general business licenses are required by your city or state to allow you to start doing business. This business structure makes it very simple to pay your taxes because the income from the business is considered personal income, and you simply attach a Schedule C Form to your standard 1040. You will be able to write off much of your income as business expenses (with proper proof, such as business receipts) and very likely be able to take many legitimate business deductions. While there is much less hassle involved in terms of formalities and paperwork, there is also a downside to being a sole proprietor. You are tied to the business. This means that if someone sues your company, they are, in effect, suing you personally. This could potentially raise your insurance costs and wreak havoc on your personal assets.

If you incorporate, you can shield your personal assets from the risk of lawsuits. While this is not always 100 percent the case, incorporating typically takes the onus off of you personally. By incorporating, the business becomes a separate entity, and an individual can sue the business as opposed to suing you personally, thus allowing you to better protect your personal assets.

Along with the advantages to incorporating, comes much more paperwork, more record-keeping, and many more requirements you need to follow, such as keeping minutes of your staff meetings. Tax situations also differ, and you need to discuss with your accountant the best manner of avoiding double taxation on the same money—once by the corporation and once on your personal income taxes.

If you decide to go into business with a partner, you should have a partnership agreement, created with the help of an attorney. This is a little more complicated than a sole proprietorship but is still easier to set up than a corporation. You get some of the same advantages with a partnership that you do with a sole proprietorship—ease of setup, little bureaucratic decision making required, and a direct income from your business. However, there is a downside. At least one of you, if not both, will be completely liable for any risks associated with a business.

Another problem occurs when one partner decides he or she wants out—there goes your partnership. You then have to restructure the business as a sole proprietorship or find another partner. But perhaps the biggest disadvantage is that you generally have to stand by any agreements your partner makes. This can be dangerous if your partner isn't someone you

Bright Idea

Want to know more about incorporating? Business Filings (www.bizfilings.com) details the ins and outs for you, with a checklist of questions to ask your lawyer and price points for comparison with local legal services. For a few hundred dollars, Business Filings will even do the paperwork for you.

completely trust or if you and your partner have different visions of the company or different personal goals. Make sure you discuss all long-range plans with a partner and determine ahead of time how much time, money, and effort each party will put into the business. If it's not going to be a 50–50 split, determine that ahead of time and make sure you are both comfortable with your roles, so resentment does not follow. And be very careful if you plan to go into business with a relative. Make sure you can separate business from a personal relationship.

Limited liability corporations, or LLCs, can provide the best of both worlds as a somewhat "hybrid" solution. The owners of an LLC have the liability protection of a corporation. Just like a corporation, the LLC exists as a separate entity. There are also fewer requirements with an LLC. A couple of drawbacks, however, are that an LLC dissolves when one partner dies or goes bankrupt, where a corporation can go on forever. Also, they are more complex to set up than a sole proprietorship or a partnership, but less complicated than starting a corporation. Additionally, LLCs are fairly new and not an option in all states, so you will have to find out about an LLC in your state of business.

You can also set up an S Corporation, which is similar to an LLC. The principal organizational differences between the two relate to the somewhat more favorable and simpler way LLCs report taxes and to the ability of an S Corporation to offer stock and set up Employee Stock Option Plans (ESOPs), which help in hiring employees. Just about everything about an S Corpation requires a good deal more regulatory paperwork.

LLCs are easier for the one- or two-person company to keep up. LLCs are probably an especially good idea as partnership vehicles because they offer more flexibility in parceling out ownership and participation of principals than some alternatives.

Just remember, the type of structure for your business is a decision you should not make without consulting an attorney. He can take into account your particular circumstances and recommend the structure that's right for you.

A lawyer can also can help you navigate local license and regulatory requirements. You're bound to incur some minor expense for business and tax permits—how minor depends on your municipality and state. If you need any special permits or licenses, a lawyer can tell you.

On the bean-counting side, you may well have to collect sales tax and file the quarterly

Tip...

Smart Tip

Keep your business taxes, especially payroll taxes, current. No one else—not the most aggressive credit card lender—levies interest on overdue accounts as quickly as Uncle Sam, and no one else has as good a chance of collecting. Even if you're a limited liability corporation and go bankrupt, the IRS and state tax authorities can hold you personally liable for these taxes plus penalties, forever.

paperwork involved in that. You may also have a payroll. After working out the initial setup, these functions are carried forward by your accountant. You can easily contract with a payroll service or hire a part-time bookkeeper and have them make all the necessary deductions. As for quarterly taxes to different entities and your year-end tax obligations, these activities may involve an hour or two worth of your accountant's time per quarter and a little more at year-end.

Create a Full-Powered Business Plan

While you brainstorm your business name and mission statement, you should start to flesh out the details of your business plan. This plan is a living document that you revise frequently as your knowledge of your market, opportunities, and abilities grow. Revising is good, especially in the early days. It's a sign of healthy growth in your understanding. Also, it may be tough to get a handle on many of the plan elements at first—particularly the forward-looking income statement. Don't worry. You'll get better at it as you go.

The business plan serves two principal purposes. First, it gives you a document that you can show potential investors and partners that encapsulates your venture and its prospects. Second, it serves as a blueprint or touchstone for you to use in the organization and running of your company. As your company changes, your business plan and mission statement should change with it to more accurately reflect your market opportunities.

Although it is a somewhat complicated document, you don't need to have previous experience writing a business plan. For an inexpensive jump start, try one of several plan-writing programs such as Business Resource Software's Business Plan Write (www.brs-inc.com) or Palo Alto Software's Business Plan Pro (www.paloalto.com). Versions sell for $100 to $150 and are much easier to revise and much more cohesive than patching together the necessary spreadsheets and word processing documents. These packages offer templates into which you can pour your own words and numbers. They are designed by experts in marketing, planning, and strategy. Most automatically generate the proposal letters, budgets, financial charts, and other documents you'll need. Bplan.com (www.bplan.com) is a great place to read up on, and find samples of, business plans (they also market Business Plan Pro).

Here's a quick list of the major elements any business plan should contain:

- *Executive summary*. This is where you encapsulate your entire plan into one page compelling enough to get people to read the rest of the plan. Often this is written last, after having created and written the entire business plan, making it easier to summarize.

- *Industry overview.* Study the industry as a whole, in this case online education, then outline what is happening in the industry and how you can find a niche.
- *The company.* Give a brief synopsis of your company's goals, and include your one-paragraph mission statement.
- *Problem/solution.* What is the market need you're trying to satisfy? What's unique about your solution?
- *Operational overview.* How will your business operate? Explain the manner in which you will function: from students paying for courses through the manner in which your courses will be delivered. Also include whether you will be accredited, provide certification, etc. This section should provide the reader, and you as an entrepreneur, with a clear understanding of the process by which the business will operate.
- *The market.* Describe your target market in as much detail as possible and try to quantify its growth potential. Make it clear who you are planning to reach, and don't say "everyone." Most businesses do not appeal to everyone.
- *Competitive analysis.* Describe who else is in the market, how successful they are, and why they are successful. Include how they differ from you and what competitive edge you can offer. Be honest in your evaluations of other businesses and do not try to show why you will "be the best, and run everyone else out of business." Be realistic and show why you can gain a market share of the overall demographic audience.
- *Your marketing plan.* The marketing plan is an important aspect of your overall business and one to which you need to pay strict attention. Are you planning to advertise? Will you use direct mail? Special promotions? Web site optimization? Also, if you have media contacts or know of publicists that will help you spread the word, include that information in this section. The mere process of writing this section gets you motivated to work on this important area. Remember, building a great online learning web environment does not mean that people will come. Therefore, you need to explain (especially to investors) how you will drive business to your web site.
- *Financial statements.* Provide a three-to-five-year forecast of revenues and expenses. Work hard on this one with your accountant—it can be an eye-opener for everyone, including yourself. Be diligent and *realistic*. When making projections, lean toward conservative estimates. Use charts, graphs, and financial statements to support this section.
- *Biographies.* This may be your strongest drawing card. Describe your background and the backgrounds of the key participants in the business. Include their unique qualifications that will help achieve the company goals. Don't overdo this section—bios should not be more than two or three paragraphs or

a page at the most. Leave out extraneous matter such as your Boy Scout merit badge. You'd be surprised at how much people will include about themselves, much of which has nothing to do with the business at hand.

At the end of the business plan, include all pertinent documents (including financial statements) that add to the merit of the overall document. Before you show a business plan to any potential investors, review it carefully, rewrite anything that is not clear, make sure you have covered all of the bases, and proofread for errors. Finally, put a table of contents up front and a cover page.

Be Sure to Insure

You need business insurance, if only for the simple fact that nowhere is American ingenuity more amply demonstrated than in the legal profession. We are in the most litigious time in American history, with lawsuits flying in and out of the courts. Dealing with the public is fraught with liability potential. Therefore, you'll need to figure on buying a $1 million worth of business liability insurance for an annual premium of around $1,500, depending on the provider. The amount has as much to do with the way insurance is priced as with how much you might need—there's a relatively high initial buy-in. You can buy less, but you'll only save a few dollars a year, so you may as well have the peace of mind. Some of your business partners may require that you carry even more business insurance.

You'll need health insurance for yourself and a health plan with workers' compensation insurance if you have employees. You'll also want fire insurance for your office or home office. If you're working from home, check your homeowners policy and inquire about getting a rider. If you work in a flood plain, on the side of a volcano, or on the side of any mountain, you may need additional riders.

Where Credit's Due

If you're offering your e-learning customers academic credits or certifications, they need to know you are the real deal, so you must offer suitable accreditation. No matter how great your courses are, how skilled your instructors may be, how professional looking your web site, or even how successful you are in getting your students jobs, the world is looking for parchment, paper, a diploma, a certificate, or another sign of legitimacy. If you're operating an online university, this is particularly important.

Most traditional colleges and universities are accredited by one of a handful of formal accreditation bodies, and most online universities are similarly accredited. While accreditation can take several years to obtain, it is well worth the wait because it provides you with that necessary degree of legitimacy and elevates your status as a learning institution.

Granted, not every institution, online or not, is accredited, and there is no legal requirement that accreditation be obtained. Many colleges operate for quite some time before achieving accreditation. But a degree from an unaccredited institution is often considered much less valuable in the job market, and it may even seem downright fraudulent to some.

After all, anybody can open a business, get a fictitious business name statement, and call themselves a university. And anyone can create his or her own accrediting organization. The Council for Higher Education Accreditation (www.chea.org) keeps watch on such organizations. It looks out for such things as "diploma mills," schools that make it very easy to earn a diploma, even if it is a fairly meaningless piece of paper.

Some such web sites make it easy to earn a degree in a very limited amount of time, while others give degrees based on an often unvalidated description of life experiences. These types of "school" are actually not new and not limited to the online environment. Brick-and-mortar diploma mills dispensing bogus degrees and diplomas still exist and date back to the late 1800s.

Therefore, it is important to take the time and make the effort toward accreditation if you want to fulfill the needs of students seeking degrees. While waiting, make sure you are offering courses in conjunction with the requirements set forth by the necessary governing bodies. Trying to cut corners or find shortcuts to providing a full and legitimate education will probably come back to haunt you once word gets out, and can be disastrous for your company.

Different forms of higher education often require different forms of accreditation, and even if you're an online business taking in students from all over the world, you're subject to the laws of the district where you are physically running your business. Every state seems to take a different tack. Each has an agency that oversees higher education, which you can find in the government pages of your phone book. There is, for example, an "Indiana Commission for Higher Education" and a "California Postsecondary Education Commission." These and similar agencies are the best places to start learning about what procedures you have to go through to operate in your state and become accredited.

At the highest level, six regional associations handle college accreditation:

1. *Middle States Association of Colleges and Schools* (www.msache.org). For Delaware, District of Columbia, Maryland, New Jersey, New York, Pennsylvania, Puerto Rico, and the Virgin Islands
2. *New England Association of Schools and Colleges* (www.neasc.org). For Connecticut, Maine, Massachusetts, New Hampshire, Rhode Island, and Vermont

3. *North Central Association of Colleges and Schools* (www.ncacihe.org). For Arizona, Arkansas, Colorado, Illinois, Indiana, Iowa, Kansas, Michigan, Minnesota, Missouri, Nebraska, New Mexico, North Dakota, Ohio, Oklahoma, South Dakota, West Virginia, Wisconsin, and Wyoming
4. *Northwest Commission of Colleges and Universities* (www.nwccu.org). For Alaska, Idaho, Montana, Nevada, Oregon, Utah, and Washington
5. *Southern Association of Colleges and Schools* (www.sacs.org). For Alabama, Florida, Georgia, Kentucky, Louisiana, Mississippi, North Carolina, South Carolina, Tennessee, Texas, and Virginia
6. *Western Association of Schools and Colleges* (www.wascweb.org). For American Samoa, California, Hawaii, and Guam

Some schools are also accredited by professional accrediting agencies. For example, law schools are accredited by the American Bar Association (www.abanet.org) and medical schools by the American Medical Association (www.ama-assn.org) or the Association of American Medical Colleges (www.aamc.org). Computer science schools may be accredited by the Computing Sciences Accreditation Board (www.csab.org) and engineering schools by the Accrediting Board for Engineering and Technology (www.abet.org).

The story is different outside academia. If you're providing courses that lead to students gaining computer accreditation or certification, such as the MCSE (Microsoft Computer System Engineer), you will need accreditation from Microsoft or the vendor whose products are the topic of the courses.

9

Putting Your Money Down

In this chapter, we discuss some of the typical start-up costs you can expect when setting up various types of online businesses. We consider the pros and cons of having a homebased business vs. working out of commercial office space. We also look at how some of the entrepreneurs we interviewed got their start in business and offer some tips for saving money.

Penny Pinching

There are many different ways to go into the online education business. Each has its own infrastructure and expense requirements. Different entrepreneurs do the same thing in different ways. Are you someone disciplined enough to operate from a home office, or are there so many distractions in your household that you can't wait to leave for a quieter office environment every morning? Are you dipping a toe in the water with an informational web portal or are you going full bore with an online university or highly transactional web site complete with shopping cart?

The growth component in your five-year plan is a factor in your expenses, too. Many online learning companies start very modestly and then grow very rapidly—that is, those that survive. There's no standard cookie-cutter list of start-up expenses. Instead, we'll give an overview of common scenarios and the expenses involved, and provide some planning tools.

As always, money is the driving factor in many start-up decisions. We assume you want to get the ball rolling spending as little as possible. If you aren't concerned about your start-up capital, you should be. No matter how much you have, there will be unbudgeted surprises around nearly every corner, and cash isn't likely to start flowing as soon as you think it will. (And remember that you've got your own living expenses in the meantime.) Successful entrepreneurs emphasize that fiscal discipline fosters a kind of ingenuity and operating discipline that puts them in good standing when those inevitable challenges arise. Financial problem solving is a boot camp of sorts for training the mind in creative sales and marketing solutions.

"For an object lesson in what happens when cash-rich companies pursue the opposite strategy, just look at the first wave of dotcoms," notes Ed Harris, co-founder of Precision Information, a personal financial education firm. Super Bowl TV ads, fancy office space, and corporate perks didn't help at all when these companies couldn't convert page clicks, viral marketing, and other New Economy revenue models into receivables. "Having money isn't the only answer to the business challenges you'll face," says Harris, who has been involved in six start-up ventures, including Persoft, one of the nation's most successful software companies, in the late 1980s. "With Persoft, we were all totally inexperienced. But we were fortunate—and I mean fortunate—that we didn't

Tip...

Smart Tip

Purchase computer and other office equipment in dollar amounts that will allow you to expense the total on your tax return, rather than depreciating it. The precise dollar amount will vary with your projected tax obligations for a given year; consult your accountant. But expensing equipment saves paperwork and almost always provides more tax advantage than depreciating it.

Dollar Stretcher

Don't lease office space—sublet. The commercial real estate market swings between scarcity and glut fairly rapidly. Even in times of scarcity, companies with long-term leases overestimate their space needs or suffer reversals of fortune. Search out distress cases in the classified ad sections of local newspapers, advertisers, or professional journals. Just make sure that subleasing is allowed on the original lease.

have any money at all, so we could bootstrap slowly and learn the discipline of running the business lean. These are skills people just don't learn if they have a lot of money in the bank."

Harris recalls a cross-town competitor with great technology and enough venture capital funding that it didn't need to develop those management skills. The competitor lasted a year, while Harris' company, profitable in its first year and every year thereafter, survived to grow to $22 million in annual revenues before Harris sold it. Harris sought, then turned down, venture capital money when the venture capitalists insisted on giving him twice what he needed on the condition he grow twice as fast as he wanted. So even if you've just landed a big chunk of VC cash—or more likely an option on a big chunk of VC cash—try to spend as little as possible. Remember, you can't reach into someone else's wallet without giving up some control of your company.

"Innovate, invent your own approaches, and never take the first price offered to you for anything," says Mark Carey, founder of training software reseller MySoftwareHelper. Carey never pays "list" for anything—not a car, a lawyer, or a box of office supplies at Costco. He shops around and uses the price he gets from one supplier to negotiate with another. "It's absolutely amazing what people will do to get your business," he says. "But if you don't ask, you'll pay full sticker price or worse."

Down Home or Downtown

Precision Information has brought financial education to a million individuals and partnered with some of the largest software and financial services companies in the country. Its four equity partners work out of a modest office—an office that doesn't see the partners very often.

LearnKey, one of the largest nationwide providers of e-learning content, started in its owner's basement. Most of the resellers who now sell LearnKey's courseware to corporations, and sometimes sell a hundred or a thousand copies or licenses of the courseware at a time, are still one or two people operating from home.

The husband and wife team of John Henry and Linda Cassleman, who run CourseBridge, featuring some 50 courses in writing, computing, instructor training, spirituality, and more, are still based in their Ontario, Canada, home, where they set up shop some seven years ago.

Most online educational opportunities can be germinated in a home office. Some will require a move to greater space in a dedicated office location, while others will thrive from a well appointed (or at least comfortable) home office. Mark Carey worked as a sales representative and consultant from a home office for two decades. But when he started MySoftwareHelper, he knew that he needed a small office, both because broadband internet service wasn't available in his rural Washington hometown and because he knew he would need to hire a couple of critical employees early on. (One was hired for technical expertise, the other for experience selling into the education and government markets.)

As we go deeper into the age of communications, the traditional constraints of time and space begin to disappear. Even the largest clients are comfortable doing business with operations whose corporate headquarters is a basement, back bedroom, or even a kitchen table. Usually, they never know. The influx of broadband and wireless connections into the home market over the past five years has made it very possible to bring what was once seen as "office" equipment into your home environment. Of course, you can always spread out by setting up a small office close to home. Spry Learning is doing $4 million annually and operating a nationwide training network that reaches thousands of seniors from a small office in downtown Portland.

The price of office space and utilities, of course, vary widely depending on whether you are in a small town or major city. Flexibility of lease terms vary with the availability of office space in your town. If you have a space that permits you to work from home, you obviously have reduced your start-up costs to a small amount for office equipment and a small delta above your current living expenses. While commercial real estate may be cheap in North Sioux City, South Dakota (where Gateway Computer started), even the tiniest commercial space in San Francisco or New York can be very costly. One of the positive factors when seeking space for this type of business is that your office location need not be in a prestigious building or a bustling neighborhood, since clients and customers are not coming to your door. You can, therefore, be situated in an off-the-beaten track location as long as you feel it is safe. Then, you can always arrange to meet a new instructor at a restaurant for a luncheon or at a similar neutral location, if necessary.

With some due diligence, you may find some great deals in what are typically higher rent locations by partnering with a current inhabitant. Mark Carey found extremely nice digs in a lawyer's office in downtown Tacoma, Washington, by looking for a firm in a bind. As luck would have it, he found a law firm with too many offices on its hands and a five-year lease. He got a two-room office with all the amenities, including a large communal conference room, with all utilities paid for $400 a month.

Often, businesses that are downsizing have some extra space available. Conversely, young start-ups, that may have taken on more space than they can fill, may also have space available. It's worth checking out all options. Be flexible when looking for office space. Remember, your key concerns should be cost and connectivity—you need to be hooked up to the internet at all times. We'll talk more about commercial office space later. First, let's quote Dorothy, "There's no place like home."

Home Base

Much has been written about how to actually set up a home office. You'll find books and web sites that will help you with everything from low cost shelving to Feng Shui. One key to home office success is to carve out a dedicated space in your home. That minimizes interruptions and lets you mentally shift from home life to work life.

Naturally, you will need the usual array of office equipment—phone, personal computer, printer, scanner, and copier, plus office furniture including a desk or computer table (or both), desk chair, and filing cabinet(s). You may choose to buy a printer, scanner, and copier separately, or you might opt for a multifunction device. There are pros and cons to each: a multifunction device is probably cheaper and saves space, but you'll probably give up some flexibility in choosing the features you want. Additionally, when one function stops working, you usually lose all of your functions at once. Since faxes are becoming less common in the age of e-mail, you can usually get a fax program and use your phone line to switch to fax mode when the occasional fax comes in. A quality, reliable printer is more important today than a fax feature, so seek out the better printer for a few dollars more. In the end you'll be glad you did.

The "Homebased Start-Up Expenses" worksheet on page 100 shows a sample first-year outlay for an online business operating out of a home office. It also suggests some of the issues to consider in getting this type of business started.

The biggest concerns when working from home are:

- *Limited or NO distractions*. This means finding a location where you will not be interrupted by other activities going on in the home. It also means selecting hours where you will not be expected to handle nonwork related responsibilities. The advantage of a home office is that you negate commuting time, which allows you to go back into your office at midnight or other "off hours" to work for a while if you so choose.
- *Proper wiring*. Today, this also means proper wireless features if you choose to set up a wireless system for your computer. A business that is dependant on web interaction cannot use a dial-up connection. In fact, you need the most reliable, high-speed internet hook up that you can afford. This is the lifeline of your

Homebased Start-Up Expenses Worksheet

Equipment	Estimate	Actual
Phone lines (1 phone with two lines, 1 cell phone)	$3,000	
Utilities (above and beyond home use)	400	
High-speed internet access	600	
Basic office equipment and furniture	1,000	
A PC	1,200	
A laptop computer	800	
Laser printer	500	
Software (office suite, security, fax, accounting)	1,600	
Dedicated web site (web design and hosting)	2,000	
Insurance (fire, health, personal liability)	5,000	
Legal and accounting services (incorporation, trademark search, contract review, tax filings)	3,000	
Licenses/permits	250	
Subscriptions to trade journals	100	
Association membership dues	300	
Advertising/marketing	5,000	
Miscellaneous supplies	500	
Total Start-Up Expenses	**$25,250**	

business. Also, make sure to select an area of the house with enough outlets for your computer, peripherals, and any other electronic devices you may need.

- *Backing yourself up*. Let's face it, how many people are diligent and back up their work on their computer hard drives on a regular basis? Very few! In many large companies, the IT crew is running backups of your corporate data for you. In your own business, you are responsible for backing up your database, and doing so often. It takes only one power surge for you to lose your enrollment database. Companies like Overland Storage (www.overlandstorage.com), Quantum (www.quantum.com), among others, offer electronic storage and other solutions to save your data in case of emergencies, such as fire, theft, or natural disaster.

Many stories are told by companies in the New Orleans area about the aftermath of Katrina. Some businesses were able to recover and resume normal activities because all of their vital data was stored off site, either electronically or physically. Other companies lost thousands of dollars and spent numerous hours trying to recreate such data, and were often unable to do so. It is imperative that you back up your system database as well as your student, teacher, and course information. Even if you just use a couple of CDs and back up your system every other day, storing one in your home and one in your safety deposit

Suite Software Success

To start off, you'll need the standard office productivity applications—word processor, spreadsheet, database, desktop presentation, and scheduling software. You can buy an office suite and have this covered in basic form. For example, Microsoft Office Professional sells for between $500 and $600, depending on where and how you buy it. In some cases, you may have Office bundled with a new PC. However, also popular and far less expensive are Corel WordPerfect Office and Lotus SmartSuite.

Even if you use an accountant, you should still track your income and expenses in your own accounting program such as Intuit's QuickBooks (www.intuit.com) or a small business-oriented personal finance manager like Quicken Home & Business. Never leave too much responsibility in the hands of someone else, especially when it comes to handling your money. Pay attention.

You'll also need to protect yourself from attack with a robust anti-virus, firewall, intrusion-detection package, such as Zone Alarm Professional from Zone Labs or the anti-virus software packages from PC-cillin, McAfee, or Bitdefender from Softwin. This is not the place to skimp on spending—you could lose far more money than you'll save. Buy a top-of the line firewall and anti-virus program.

Don't be tempted to save money by copying software programs. It's illegal, you are increasingly likely to get caught, and the financial penalties could put you out of business.

box, you will know you are covered. Backing up your business data is as important as having insurance.

Beware!

Be sure to keep business and personal expenses separate. Entrepreneurs who mingle business and personal cash often run into trouble with the flow of both. The easiest way to keep the two separate is with separate credit cards for business expenses, downloaded into finance or accounting software such as Quicken Home & Business or QuickBooks. Also save receipts in two separate places

Your other major budget item will be marketing: advertising, public relations, and promotions. Customers don't just appear—you must go and gather them, and then keep them. Your marketing approach will vary by the audience you're trying to reach. You'll need to make a concerted effort to hone in on your target audience and spend money carefully. The key is to spread the word about your web site by getting the most bang for your buck. Find appropriate links and trade with other businesses. Use viral marketing by making it easy for anyone who registers for a course to register a friend for half price. Look for inexpensive places to run constant targeted ads. The key is to develop a full marketing plan. Marketing is discussed in more detail later in the book. For now, figure anywhere from 10 to 20 percent of your budget, maybe more, will go to marketing. Just remember, this is an arbitrary figure because budgets vary tremendously by company.

Picks in Commercial Space

Your start-up may be too ambitious or too logistically complex to launch in a home office; if so, start-up costs may be considerably greater. For example, you may prefer to deliver your IT online educational content in a physical classroom with a network of PCs. You may create sophisticated coursework with a team of developers or launch an online university or another more substantial initiative that requires traditional office space. More complex computer equipment, along with skilled technical people to run it, require that you have more space.

Most of your first-year expenses will include the same budget items you would incur when setting up a homebased business. But there are some very expensive differences.

Surprisingly, office space may not be the most onerous of them, depending on how the commercial space market in your area is doing and or how large a classroom you will need. You probably won't need a lot of space to start. We use a moderately priced office of $600 a month on the accompanying "Commercial Office Start-Up Expenses"

Dollar Stretcher

Cut your phone expenses by signing up for a cell phone plan that includes no long-distance or roaming charges. Use your cell phone for most long-distance and toll calls. You may also get a discount on landline or long-distance calls from a provider with both cellular and landline business.

worksheet on page 104 for the typical first-year outlay for an online education business run out of commercial space. Change that as necessary for your locale.

The larger the business, the more likely you will need a number of networked computers. Have someone with experience setting up a computer network get you started and make sure you have his phone number for troubleshooting. Networks do go down from time to time, and you need to get them up and operational as soon as possible.

Depending on what you're offering, your web site could cost a few hundred dollars or a few hundred thousand. Such vagaries and options make it difficult to offer a cookie-cutter budget.

Remember, you can give yourself greater liability protection by incorporating. Once you take on actual office space, a classroom, or registration area where customers can walk into your business environment, the chance of liability goes up enormously from the home office situation.

For marketing, we'll stick with 10 to 15 percent of your overall budget. Beyond the web site, you may want to advertise in professional or association journals or other publications, make appearances at conferences or trade shows, or find other venues.

Don't forget memberships in professional associations such as the American Society of Training and Development (www.astd.org) or the U.S. Distance Learning Association (www.usdla.org), which offer many benefits for online education businesses.

If utilities aren't bundled, you've got bills that will depend on your location. Heating, cooling, and lights can vary from $75 a month in the summertime to $500 during winter months in cold climates. We've estimated an annual total of $3,300. But you can get a much more precise estimate easily just by adding up a year's worth of utility bills for your home and adding, say, another 25 percent for every employee in your office. While most of your business utility expense is already accounted for in your home utility bills (with just a little extra if you have a home office), it's a separate expense if you rent commercial space.

You should have a broadband internet connection with at least a DSL connection, or T1 if you're hiring more than a handful of people or running a public web server yourself. It's typically cheaper and far more effective, however, to have your web computer infrastructure hosted by a company in that business. It can provide the necessary security, backup, and environmental controls as well as immediate scalability to keep pace with your web site growth.

Commercial Office Start-Up Expenses Worksheet

Equipment	Estimate	Actual
Rent	$7,200	
Phone lines (2 landlines, 2 cell phones)	4,000	
Utilities	3,300	
High-speed internet access	1,000	
Basic office equipment and furniture	3,500	
2 PCs, one server	3,000	
2 laptops	3,000	
Laser printer	500	
Software (office suite, security, fax accounting, networking)	3,200	
Web site design/development	27,000	
Web hosting	1,200	
Insurance (fire, health, personal liability)	8,000	
Legal/accounting services (incorporation, trademark registration, contract review, quarterly taxes)	4,000	
Licenses/permits	250	
Subscriptions to trade journals	100	
Association membership dues	300	
Advertising/marketing	17,000	
Payroll services	1,800	
Payroll and benefits (for two employees)	80,000	
Miscellaneous supplies	500	
Total Start-Up Expenses	**$168,850**	

Beware!

Selling online education courses is no marketing panacea. One online learning courseware provider, which anticipated annual revenues of $150,000 when it launched its highly professional, interactive web site a couple years ago, has only been able to generate around $5,000 annually so far. As always, you must find potential customers and actually close the sales.

To do business over your web site, your costs will be more significant. E-commerce sites are more complex both on the front and back end. They require sophisticated databases on the back end and thoughtful and professional design elements on the front. Design elements and back-end programming are best left to professionals. If that's not you, put your effort into selecting the right professionals.

Mark Carey of MySoftwareHelper paid $30,000 to an ad agency for creative work on his site and $19,000 to a pair of web designers and programmers to build his site. He is convinced that he got a bargain. He shopped around for months and got estimates of up to $250,000. And the proposals often included monthly service fees. Carey insisted that his web site designers provide easy-to-use templates so he could update his site himself.

Like any business, you'll need insurance—at least $1 million in business liability insurance for a cost of somewhere around $1,500. You can buy less, but you won't save much.

You'll also need health insurance for at least one employee—you. Figure $250 a month or $3,000 a year for an HMO plan that just covers you. As you probably are aware, health costs can be all over the map, depending on your age, locale, and whether you're covering family members or setting up an employee plan.

Bottom line: Except for a little more computer hardware and a fancy web site if needed, the cost of setting up an online education business probably doesn't vary that much from most other sales and service-oriented concerns that require some degree of expertise. Also note that, as with any entrepreneurial venture, you may earn little or no revenue in the first year because your costs will be greater than your income. Have faith, it takes most new businesses anywhere from one to three or four years to have any noticeable profit.

10

Content and Delivery

Here we focus on two of the most critical elements of any online learning business: content and how it is delivered. We take a look at the options for developing or buying course content, as well as the various methods you can choose to deliver that content to your customers. Some of this was touched upon in Chapter 7, when we took a closer look at instructors.

As noted earlier, online learning can cover any topic for which there is a paying customer (and that customer isn't always the student). It can be canned or live, as simple as text on an HTML page or as complicated as training simulations for astronauts. Content can be built with tools ranging from a word processor to a course management system to Macromedia Flash to a thousand distinctive software platforms. Delivery can be set up to work in any way a computer accepts content. So don't expect a cookie-cutter guide!

Content Is King

Content is, and always has been, king. But it has a troubled reign. While there are outstanding courses being developed all the time, online education content still has a lot of room to improve. That spells O-P-P-O-R-T-U-N-I-T-Y for would-be content creators. It's also something of a hurdle for the sellers of online learning services, especially among corporate or institutional customers who might have experienced inferior courseware in the past.

Course content is inextricably linked to the way it is delivered—both delivery mechanisms and that indefinable quality known as "teaching." Delivery can be in real-time in a synchronous course led by an instructor, at the student's convenience over a few weeks or months in a course delivered asynchronously via instructor, or totally self-directed and self-paced, or in some combination of these.

Each approach has different appeals in different ways as we discussed earlier. People prefer to learn in different ways. Some people are readers, some are viewers, and some need a hands-on experience. One strategy for coping with these preferences is to provide multiple delivery options.

Remember that if you are creating content with your own user interface, you need feedback on the user interface from people who are not involved in the development of the course. The user interface must be both easy to learn and efficient to run. Software vendors may spend thousands of dollars on usability testing. You can often get a very similar reality check by finding volunteers who represent your target market and will give you honest assessments. As an incentive, you can pay them a small fee or give them a free class once your business is up and running.

You need to take the art and science of learning very seriously. Hundreds of books and articles have been written about online learning. Browsing Barnes and Noble, online or in person, or searching online education on Amazon shows you the current choices.

The wide range of subject matter and audience types to which such learning can be delivered makes it difficult to generalize about what constitutes good content and delivery. But your customers will know it when they see it.

Getting Beyond Text

"Computer training from books doesn't work," asserts Mark Carey of MySoftware Helper. "They are just far too wordy and make things far more complicated than they need to be. I am the kind of person who needs to have it shown to me as opposed to explained to me. Most people don't like to read," says Carey. That's not limited to computer training. The best online educational courseware is experiential, blending highly illustrative content—video, animation, photos, or realistic diagrams—with student interactivity. That's why LearnKey, in St. George, Utah, spends so much money to create videos of real instructors doing real things in its courseware.

Of course, online learners don't necessarily have access to a classroom, a broadband internet connection, or even a computer every minute of every day. Books, workbooks, or videos can be useful adjuncts to courseware. That's particularly true for IT courses. Many IT certificate-seekers appreciate having a hard-copy reference to go along with the certification course, which can take months to complete. One multi-certificate holder says that he always buys a $40 computer book to go along with his certification courses that can cost $800 to $2,000.

Bottom line: There isn't one road to learning, and the roads are not mutually exclusive. Finding the right blend of textual and visual content for a particular audience is not a trivial task. How well you solve it will have a lot to do with your success. "We surveyed 700 managers in 30 different industries and asked them what they're most commonly using to create online learning environments," says Jack Rochester of the Delphi Group, an IT business strategy firm. "Everybody's using books. Everybody's using CD-ROMs. Everybody's using videotapes. We found that the most common thing they were doing was using existing PowerPoint presentations." That leaves

Lend a Helping Hand

Don't assume that educators versed in traditional educational classroom modalities can immediately make the transition to online teaching without taking a ride around the learning curve. Many instructors find themselves somewhat overwhelmed or at least a bit confused when planning an online course with its different set of audio and visual needs, and interactive strategies. For these teachers, it means adjusting their change in role from the leading speaker to that of a facilitator. This means that you need to be ready to provide the necessary assistance and even some technical support.

plenty of room for improvement—and entrepreneurial opportunities.

Instruction Beyond Instructors

You can't divorce content from the content deliverer or from the delivery method. It doesn't matter how good the course is if the teacher or delivery method can't get it across. Online learning courseware frees people from the constraints of time and space and provides them an opportunity to deliver high-quality instruction to a much broader audience than is possible through traditional classroom training. A good instructor with good content can reach many more people than through traditional modalities.

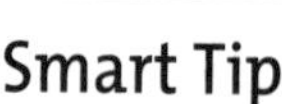

Smart Tip

Want to get an idea of just how inadequate and confusing text-based instruction can be? Click the Windows Help menu and select a topic, any topic. Note how the simplest task requires excessive explanation and steps that are made confusing by describing in words something that is meant to be seen and acted upon.

Unlike traditional courses, good online learning courseware doesn't just depend on the instructor—it's a team effort. "The most important thing is not really the interactivity or the multimedia experience," says Morten Sohlberg, who runs Sessions.edu, an online web design school based in New York City. "It's the ability of an organization to pull together a very large team of people."

"Creating a good online learning course is like making a good motion picture," says Sohlberg. While classic classrooms focus on the instructor, the best online learning methodologies bring together a group of people to create a highly specialized and creative product. The importance of the instructor is not diminished, but the talents of more specialists can be brought to bear. Content at Sohlberg's institution comes from a combination of the instructor's knowledge and research, input from other educators, and a variety of designers and producers. "The content that you're absorbing is bound to be so much better than what one person could bring to a classroom," says Sohlberg.

Of course, today, with advanced webcams and digital cameras, Sohlberg's Speilberg-esque motion picture approach to online learning is

Beware!

Watch your budget when producing videos or other complex online forms of delivering content. Many entrepreneurs have found themselves deep in debt by overdoing the web content production. While you do need quality, you also need to keep in mind your costs and limitations. Don't buy into the big buck dynamics you see on feature films and television programs and think you can do more than is possible. Be realistic—no car chases to illustrate the laws of motion and physics.

no longer necessary for presenting a quality learning experience. So, don't be discouraged. Low budget movies can, and have, been made and found their way to great box office success. Think of *Little Shop of Horrors*, *Sex Lies and Video Tape*, and *Blair Witch Project*, to name just a few. It's not about the size of the team or a huge budget, but about what you do with what you have available. Teams of two and three people have started web sites that have become extremely successful. CourseBridge is essentially a two-person effort offering first-rate courses, which produce satisfied and educated customers. It's all about creativity and ingenuity, not about how many people you have on your team.

Resale Value

Not every online learning provider is as ambitious as Sohlberg and others who create their own content. You can choose from existing content and add value as you resell it.

Sometimes content can be repurposed by combining it with material of your own. You might add study guides of your own creation, components tailored for certain customers, or other elements that enhance the experience for the student. Some content publishers make this easier to do than others.

For example, one customer for Precision Information's "Encyclopedia of Personal Finance" is a financial services consultant who uses it as a starting point to help government human resource managers explain 401(k) options to employees. Delivered via CD-ROM or server, the encyclopedia also lets employees explore other personal finance topics at their leisure. Precision Information's personal finance database is so flexible that the company can quickly produce custom courses for large financial services companies such as New York Life.

There are huge catalogs of content available on the web from numerous providers. You might choose to get the rights to resell them to institutions, use them as the basis for your syllabus in your own training center, or as the courseware for your own online learning web portal. In the latter case, your students are usually directed to the servers of the courseware provider's server—under your banner. Like eLearners, you can make a deal where you'll receive payment per inquiry or per student registration.

You can also offer more than just the courses you purchase. "We aren't selling a product,

Tip...

Smart Tip

How much should you pay a publisher for content? The discount off the retail price varies by the amount you buy and other contract conditions. In general, expect margins of 40 to 50 percent for starters. Also, make sure the publisher owns the rights to that which she is selling!

we're selling a solution," says Mark Carey of MySoftwareHelper, who delivers mostly Learn Key courseware to corporations, and government and educational institutions. "LearnKey is an outstanding course developer," Carey says. But LearnKey doesn't have a course for every topic, so Carey fills in the gaps with a couple of other brands. Neither Carey nor his account executives have a teaching background. But they can demo the products, install pilots, answer questions, and, in Carey's words, "make things happen."

> Tip...
>
> **Smart Tip**
>
> If you're training IT students to pass a certification exam dealing with a particular software vendor's content, you may have to acquire course material, study guides, and manuals from that vendor or its publishing arm. For example, Cisco Press has the inside track on Cisco hardware certification specifications long before others get that information. Such certification possibilities were discussed earlier in Chapter 5.

"Here is where other companies fall short—they don't understand that bringing a product in is only 10 percent of the job," says Carey. "You have to make sure it is used successfully, or they won't renew their license. If no one even knows it's available, what good have you done? But if everyone becomes familiar with a particular training modality, they won't want to use anything different."

MySoftwareHelper's company tagline is "The Source for Software Training Solutions." Whether you aspire to be a courseware developer, a reseller, or an instructor, it's not a bad philosophy to adopt. Clients won't be satisfied with just buying courseware or taking a class. Their training goals need to be satisfied.

Note that the list of online education resellers is much broader than you might expect, including colleges, Best Buy, Barnes and Noble, and many other outlets. You may find competition in places you don't expect (or, if you create your own content, new distribution outlets).

Grow Your Own

Precision Information co-founder Joe Saari saw a need for a database in one of the oldest and most vigorously debated areas of human knowledge. Despite the reams that have been written on financial topics, there was no single source for the many, rather sophisticated, financial topics that affect every one of us. Of those sources that came close, Saari judged that none could easily be tapped.

Saari created the *Encyclopedia of Personal Finance* to meet this need. His encyclopedia, which is really interactive courseware complete with testing, generally doesn't provide new information. Instead it rounds up time-tested financial knowledge and assembles it into one easily accessible source. This is a more difficult, risky, and

Help Wanted (Freelance)

The world is full of freelance and wannabe writers. If you're planning on hiring one of them to work on your courseware, you'll want a writer with a proven track record—not someone just out of a school or someone who's written a handful of articles for his hometown newspaper. It's helpful if you can find a writer who has written about the subject of your course. For example, if you plan to offer a course in network security, find someone who has published articles in the trade press on that topic. However, a good, well-versed freelancer should be able to do the research and put together the materials on a course. Your best bet is finding someone who knows how to write in the tone and style of your courseware in general. Research the going rate for freelancers in your area and work on a contract basis for a defined period of time, such as 12 weeks, to write up the course catalog. Then you can always start a new short-term contract for the next round of work you want written by the freelancer.

The world is also full of freelance graphic artists, programmers, and others with invaluable technical expertise. When possible, especially in the early days, get them under contract rather than hire them. If they work out and your business expands, go ahead and bring them on full time. First, however, be careful with your screening. View their portfolio and make sure you are getting someone who can handle the job and meet your deadlines.

time-consuming way to build your online learning business. You must spot a market, offer relevant expertise in the topic, and be highly skilled in all the required aspects of content creation.

Professional-quality content requires you to marshal considerable resources, including individuals with expertise from numerous disciplines. You need subject-matter experts who are the best of breed to create the material. Then you need a production arm, which can take that rough material and turn it into a product. The product must go through extensive quality testing for various computer platforms and scenarios. Then, of course, you need a distribution arm to reach out to the public.

The cost of creating a course can vary with the content, production values, and the fame of the instructor, as well as fixed start-up costs for facilities and amortized general and administrative costs for a continuing production operation.

Fact, Fiction, and Credibility

Let's face it, if your content is dated, inaccurate, or simply based on someone's misguided opinions, you may be in for a lot of credibility problems. Therefore, before you start posting courses, make sure they are thoroughly screened. Keep in mind that there will be courses, such as art interpretation, philosophy, and poli-sci, where there are not always "right" and "wrong" answers. However, if you are filling classes for the 2007 version of a computer software program, you'd better be sure your instructor is not teaching the 2005 version. The World Wide Web is filled with facts, some of which are inaccurate or dated. Be careful that your course content does not fall into those two categories.

One of the biggest advantages that you have with online education over traditional classroom education is that you can make instant changes to the curriculum. If a science textbook has Pluto listed as a planet, it remains as such until the next version comes out. You, however, can bump Pluto right out of the solar system with the click of a mouse. News, events, history, and science continue to change—keep pace with these changes in your courses.

11

It's All About the Software

An online learning business runs like any other business. Its product is learning, and it combines teaching techniques that predate Socrates with those that were invented last week. But delivering the product is all about the software. An online learning company belongs to the software community as well as the education community. You don't need to be a programmer, but you do need to be tuned into the latest in software and keep up with online learning technology as it evolves. If you're creating content, you must be comfortable managing or otherwise working with software professionals, just as you are with education and content professionals.

Before investing in any particular tool—and especially before betting your business model on a technological edge—make sure you have the financial resources, human capital, and even time to make use of it. And make sure that its deployment won't cut off any significant segment of your audience. Don't jump in too far ahead of your audience's willingness or ability to adopt technology.

In this chapter, we look at web sites, software for creating and delivering courses, and collaboration tools, including videoconferencing, e-mail, and real-time messaging. We also sketch out some technology trends.

Working the Web

You can build a "business card" web site over the weekend with tools that are probably on your computer or with templates from an internet Service Provider (ISP), who will host a business site for as little as $19 a month. At the other end of the spectrum, a full-fledged site that sells and delivers courses can cost hundreds of thousands to set up plus substantial ongoing expenses to maintain and update.

Wherever you are in this spectrum, you or your designated technical experts want to be armed with the massive arsenal of popular web tools. That includes graphics tools such as Adobe Photoshop, page-creation packages such as Microsoft FrontPage, and multimedia tools such as Adobe Acrobat Reader for distributing high-quality copies of documents, among others.

You also typically exploit standard servers, such as Apache or Microsoft web servers and SQL Server or Macromedia ColdFusion database servers. You'll also want web traffic reporting. If your site is sufficiently complex and often updated, you can check out complete content management systems, although these can be pricey. If you have straightforward e-commerce needs, look at off-the-shelf e-commerce services. Depending on how you plan to handle technical support, you can also consider chat-based support tools. You'll often want to rent rather than buy server software, as we'll discuss shortly.

Depending on your business model, you may be able to pass some or all of this heavy lifting off to a business partner, with a link from your site. For example, MySoftwareHelper offers LearnKey courses from its site that are delivered from LearnKey's servers. Most students don't know or don't care. This also is a very typical scenario for colleges who frequently contract with a courseware provider for a certain slice of the curriculum. MiraCosta College, for instance, sets up many online services for students on its own web site. But for online courses, it often finds it more convenient to use the services of another content developer.

Find a Friendly Host

You'll probably want to use a web hosting company (also known as an application service provider) during start-up and perhaps indefinitely. A hosting company maintains your online learning web site on its backed-up servers in its climate-controlled server farms. It provides all the back-end security and easily scalable connection options you may need as you grow. Of course, backing up your own data is also a safe bet, just in case. For a small- to mid-sized organization, this is very cost effective. You don't need to shell out for hardware or hire an IT administrator (whose salary may run $60,000 or more). You save time and avoid major headaches—server performance issues, viruses, and hack attacks are someone else's problem.

Companies charge as little as $25 a month for hosting, although $100 to 200 is more typical. Amounts climb rapidly depending on the kind of services you use.

Even if you outsource your hosting functions, you, or someone in your organization, will spend a certain amount of time managing your site on an ongoing basis. It's best if that doesn't require extensive work or technical skills.

Tools for the Creative Process

Online education creators use everything—word processors, graphics packages, 3D visualization tools, digital video editors, and soup-to-nuts learning management systems that cost corporations millions of dollars each year. Hundreds of vendors offer specialized tools for online learning. If you're creating content, your choice of tools may be entirely dictated by the market you serve. Institutions generally do not want to reinvent the wheel for each course. They would rather take advantage of their existing online learning infrastructures.

Sell a course to multiple colleges and you are likely to do business with a company like Blackboard (www.blackboard.com), which is one of the major players in that market. Such companies offer not just standard course creation and delivery tools but also a supporting suite of communication (such as forums and instant messaging), assessment, administration, and support components. (While definitions can be fuzzy and overlap, these are often described as course management systems, learning content management systems, or learning management systems. In general, we'll use learning management system (LMS).

On the corporate side, big software and/or training suppliers each promote their own soup-to-nuts online learning setup package. Their customers shell out for synchronous video courses and other materials that demand substantial infrastructure investments. Customers may also buy extensive suites of software that integrate content development (with multiple delivery mechanisms), communications, assessments, administration, support, and other related services. Centra Software (www.centra.com), for instance, offers a rich suite of real-time collaboration applications plus corporate "knowledge management" tools.

Bright Idea

Make yourself a stack of mini-CDs on which you can store a self-running demo of your software or services. About the size of a business card, these discs nonetheless fit in a standard CD-ROM player and hold more than 5 MB worth of data. They make great leave-behinds for your sales calls or giveaways for trade shows.

Corporations, government agencies, and nonprofit institutions all want to preserve their online learning investments. One aspect of that is to keep content separate from specific delivery platforms, so that it can still be accessed as those platforms evolve or die, or new platforms appear. The Defense Department created the SCORM (Shareable Content Object Reference Model) standard to allow this. Content created for such standards can, at least in theory, be plugged fairly easily into various delivery options: print, web, PC, handheld computer, and future platform alternatives.

Offerings that work over ubiquitous web browsers and their popular extensions such as e-mail and instant messaging, of course, reach the broadest potential groups of students.

Come Together

You don't do your best learning as a sponge. You learn best by actively interacting with teachers, experts, other students, and other resources. With sufficient investment in personnel, content, and infrastructure, online education can offer this in powerful ways—including some that conventional classrooms can't match. If you go this route, you must, of course, convince your customers on these points.

When setting up a virtual classroom, you at least need a way for students to simultaneously view the same content—whether that's videoconferencing, PowerPoint-like slides, a whiteboard, or another application. The viewing environment needs to be robust enough to give multiple people a way to comment or ask questions in an orderly fashion. These technologies are well in hand.

Synchronous learning is probably best applied to IT certification or university courses where course prices can support the cost. Asynchronous online learning typically lowers the cost. Student-teacher and student-student communications can happen through the well-established channels of e-mail, chat rooms, or bulletin boards.

In all cases, there is a learning curve, as discussed earlier, for you and your instructors. You still must reach out to students in very direct ways to make sure that they enjoy the same kind of give-and-take they would have in a real classroom.

Beyond standard e-mail, you may find a role for an e-mail discussion group, also known as a listserv system. With this, each person's comments are sent via e-mail to the entire group. It's often a part of an e-learning system such as Blackboard. If you aren't using one of these, you can check in a search engine for listserv services like Lyris List Manager (www.lyris.com).

More common is a bulletin or message board, just like the ones sprinkled over the web except that access is restricted to those in the course. Such online forums often spark lively, though slow-motion, discussions, including active participation by some who might stay silent in a physical classroom. A message board is often part of an LMS, and simple versions to add to your site can be found through any search engine.

You may also want to consider adding chat rooms or instant messaging to allow your students to interact with one another or (within certain schedules and limits) the instructor and/or teaching assistant.

Of course you need to set up rules and guidelines for list serv, chat rooms, and discussion groups. Millions of people use these forums everyday for discussing everything from the latest *American Idol* favorites to personal stories. Therefore, you need to make sure that all means of communication are used for the intended purposes: education, research, and communication among students, teachers, and/or other members of your business. Use password entry, monitored chats, and other means of maintaining a professional atmosphere at all times. Maintain the utmost privacy for student-school interactions and make sure technical help is available 24/7.

Registration

Thus far we have not discussed how students register for courses. This is e-commerce, and you will need some technical expertise when setting up your system of accepting credit cards online. Privacy is the number-one concern of nearly everyone doing any type of business over the internet. With identity theft at an all-time high, you need to make sure that encryption is in place and that you have tested the system repeatedly with your tech experts.

Bright Idea

Streaming media can be reused—a session conducted as a webinar can be recorded and then rebroadcast over and over as needed.

As mentioned earlier, your course catalog should lead to a landing page, a short page that provides more details on a course listing. For example, when you click on a course on CourseBridge, indeed on most online education providers, you find a page that offers a few paragraphs or a few sentences about the course, including its level (basic, intermediate, advanced), required materials (if any), start date, minimum technical requirements for the student, and a little information on the instructor. If your courses are coming from other institutions, you can either have a boilerplate about the school or link directly to the course page set up by the learning institution.

Once the student has looked at this page, he should be one click away from being able to register. Registration should be a simple process. You should have no barriers along the way—nor should you seek information beyond what you *need* for the registration. You can lose a lot of potential students by trying to get personal information that is none of your business. You can have optional surveys of existing students later on that can provide you with additional marketing data. But DO NOT try to grab data at the risk of losing a sale. It happens suprisingly frequently, leaving entrepreneurs perplexed as to why they are not generating more sales.

Your registration technology should immediately send a confirmation e-mail listing the course and the payment for the student's records. A student password should also be included so that he or she can access the course. Remind students never to show their password to anyone else. Also, make sure to have tech support at the click of a button in case there is a problem with registration or the confirmation does not appear.

Note: Make sure your registration form is fairly brief and easy to fill out. Test it out and have friends try it. Also make sure that if someone leaves out some data that they DO NOT have to start filling the form out all over again. This is another way to lose business very quickly. People are not happy when inconvenienced by what should be a very simple straightforward process. Work with your technical crew or use your own tech expertise to make registration seamless.

Online Learning Ecosystems

Course management systems (CMS) such as Blackboard and eCollege have become virtual fixtures on thousands of college campuses. A combination of interactive learning environment and administrative tools, a CMS enhances the classroom experience and streamlines academic logistics. Learning Management Systems (LMS) on the other hand are online learning ecosystems more commonly used in corporations.

Both types of environments include most of the same core features. But their names reveal the difference in emphasis, and each generally includes extra tools that more narrowly address the needs of their target audiences. For example, college-bound Blackboard emphasizes behind-the-scenes administrative tools for teachers to set up and administer courses. On the other hand, the highly interactive, real-time

Beware!

If you're running any sort of chat, online conversation, or message board, there may be a few bad apples participating, possibly subjecting your students to profanity, spam, or just plain harassment. That's why you want a moderated chat or message board, so you can filter out anything inappropriate. Fee-based services and software packages have basic automatic filtering capabilities plus a moderating tool, but nothing beats a human.

meetings that web environments like Centra and iLearning provide let companies save on travel costs and reduce lost employee work hours.

One of the least-anticipated features of both types of environments is the degree to which they foster student-to-student (or employee-to-employee) as well as student-teacher interaction. Sharon Senese, a Ph.D. candidate at San Jose State University, says the lack of face-to-face interaction with her instructors and other students is the one aspect of traditional classroom instruction that she misses with distance learning. But as a veteran of both Blackboard and many other online courses, Senese finds that a class or study group meeting or two per semester fills that gap. In fact, the 24/7 availability of one-to-one or one-to-many communications gives Senese greater contacts with more of her classmates than she might normally get in the typical overenrolled college course.

Chief Cook and Bottle Washer

Entrepreneurs have a can-do attitude. Good thing, too, because you often must be the chief marketing expert, salesperson, and technology guru in the early days. Can't afford to hire expensive talent to create your web site? Do it yourself.

Morten Sohlberg, chief executive of Sessions.edu (www.sessions.edu), ran all his web services from a $600 Macintosh for his first two years in business. Mark Carey of MySoftwareHelper programmed his first web site himself out of a how-to textbook. For his current, highly transactional and very complicated site, he hired an experienced web firm after six months of research. It took him awhile to find the right team to fulfill the very specific set of design and operational criteria he had created to ensure that his site was reliable and easy to change himself. Most people can master most of the tools if they are willing to put in the time like Sohlberg and Carey. Remember, that can-do attitude may require some long hours of learning before you can sell learning online.

Adding either of these technologies to your online educational site need not be difficult or costly. Again, you don't want to reinvent the wheel. There are plenty of chat programs available, many of which are very inexpensive or even free. Instant messaging has spread like web wildfire, and often replaces e-mail as the main form of internet connection for those in their teens and 20s. Because major IM systems often don't speak to each other, for now you must take pains to make sure that all your students are on the same IM system if you choose to use that tool.

These tools may be bundled in an LMS. They also are offered by application service providers such as Multicity (www.multicity.com). Make certain that the systems can save and archive transcriptions of your online patter.

Five for the Future: Technologies of Tomorrow

The companies that sell technology have a long and distinguished history of portraying each product as a cure-all for just about any business challenge. The press that covers technology often validates that notion, portraying each new development as a fait accompli on announcement day, even though a given technology's benefits may require years of hard work to realize.

Online learning technologies are often great examples of the sizzle being delivered long before the steak. Most of the technologies we are talking are already off and running, but they will increase in their usefulness as learning tools. We list five here in no particular order.

1. *Software simulations*. You can learn by plunging into a simulation that gives you problems to solve in an environment that's not the real world but does have realistic rules. It works for pilots and surgeons, and it can work for you.
2. *Personalized learning*. In related research, learning systems are evolving that study the way you learn best (movies? 3D simulations? text?) and then deliver content accordingly. This can be costly, but if you find several broad-based methods in which groups of students can learn effectively, you can at least offer some various learning structures.
3. *HD-DVD*. OK, this is a technology for today, not tomorrow. But the explosive growth of DVDs and now HD-DVDs allows you deliver high-quality video and other high-density material to tens of millions of potential students without worrying about bandwidth constraints. DVD material can be integrated with web-based content and real-time interactions for hybrid systems that feature the best of both worlds.

4. *Interactive TV.* You can offer significant interactions with very limited controls. If it spreads in the United States as it has in Europe, interactive TV will offer additional opportunities for learning.
5. *Cell phones.* No, they're not being utilized very much for learning purposes yet, but the interactive opportunities, thanks to text messaging and continually improving technologies, may improve the functionality of cell phones as a means of learning, along with other educational modalities. For example, consider a student taking a test away from his or her computer, and text messaging his or her answers.

All of these technologies, and others, will likely be utilized in the future for educational purposes. Do you hear a cash register ringing in the distance?

12

Finding the Finances

In this chapter, we cover the options for funding your online education venture. Will you need to work part time while starting up? Will you exhaust your savings and/or approach family and friends? Will you seek the participation of private investors? Perhaps, you will try to hit a home run with venture capital. Of course, there is always a loan from the bank or another lending institution. Then too, the Small Business Administration gets behind many small businesses with their funding plans.

Who Are You Going to Call?

The fuel of capitalism is capital. Originally intended by economist Adam Smith to refer to capital equipment—machinery, supplies, and other real assets that contribute to productivity—the term now refers to the money you invest to start and expand your business.

Although many a business starts on a shoestring and thrives, many more flounder because they don't have enough cash to see them through until revenues regularly exceed expenses. The start-up period for a business can last years. The larger the idea and the greater the potential reward, the longer the period required to feed a business before it really takes off.

Below are five ways of backing your new business.

1. *Personal assets*. Your first source is your own cash, savings, or inheritance. Many businesses have also been launched on credit cards or loans against a home mortgage. These are tremendously bad ideas. Nonetheless, most potential investors want to know that you're putting your own resources on the line before they share theirs. Therefore, you need to establish savings or a fund specifically for launching your business. Money for such a venture needs to be savings beyond your budget for day-to-day expenses and monthly bill paying.
2. *Loans*. Sure it's difficult to get a lending institution to simply hand you money unless you are ready and willing to put up collateral. You also need to convince a lender that you have a solid business plan and the skills, experience, and know-how to make the business work. Additionally, you should begin bolstering your credit rating in advance of venturing into a meeting with a lender. To do this, make sure you are caught up on your bill paying and any other outstanding loans. Then make sure the three major credit bureaus know it. The Small Business Administration can be a great source of information on loans, and it has loan programs.
3. *Friends and family*. These are the folks who know you best. While it will severely test these relationships, this is also a common source of funds for the seed phase of a venture when the basic concept is being hammered out. At the very least, you'll get practice pitching your business plan. Even if your immediate circle doesn't invest, the people in it may tell somebody who will. Make sure you have everything in writing and make sure you also discuss the potential emotional impact of borrowing from friends and family. No hard feelings?

4. *Angels*. An angel is a wealthy individual who sees value in your concept and may invest time as well as money in your project. Young entrepreneurs often overlook the value of the former, but an angel with business experience and/or knowledge of your industry can often save you more than money by helping you avoid costly mistakes. However, you need to determine the involvement of an angel in advance. If someone is going to lend you money with so many strings attached that you become a puppet, then it might not be a good fit for you and your business. Some angels give good advice, but take an otherwise hands-off approach. Make sure you feel comfortable with the angel with whom you are flying.
5. *Venture capital*. A venture capitalist is in it for the money. He or she often wants a large equity stake or even partial control of your business in exchange for bankrolling it. VCs have their choice of deals. They require a rather high minimum investment to make it worth their while and a relatively aggressive exit strategy—that is, a relatively early payback. They are interested in innovative businesses and often looking for extensive growth potential. Because there are so many possibilities and business entrepreneurs approaching VCs, they can afford to be quite selective.

There are no unbreakable rules here. Any of these investors might underwrite an online learning venture at any stage. But venture capitalists are rarely your best choice for the earliest rounds of financing. They expect to see a very well-honed business plan. They also require strong evidence—perhaps, in the form of a working software prototype or even a revenue stream—that your concept has a potentially large financial payoff. In any case, financing is only the first of many tests of your persistence and belief in your idea.

Another option is to go into cahoots with another learning establishment, offering an online arm of an existing educational business. This may help provide you with funding, although you may have some parameters to adhere to. If, however, you are the educational arm of another type of business, you may then be able to have more say in how your part of the business is built and run.

Put It on Paper

Entrepreneurs commonly struggle to get others to see what they see. It's as if entrepreneurs are a race of optimists dropped into a land of pessimists. Most people interpret as insurmountable obstacles the very circumstances that you consider opportunities or welcome barriers to the entry of competitors. Even the most experienced business types are likely to play devil's advocate when approached with an idea that will separate them from their cash for several years. You must bridge these differences in perspective with your own enthusiasm, commitment, and a very well-written, honed (and rewritten) business plan. Even if you're approaching family members, you must commit your vision to paper in such a way that others can see its possibilities. You can refer back to the discussion on business plans in Chapter 8.

> **Tip...**
>
> **Smart Tip**
>
> The first thing investors look for in a business plan is an exit strategy—how and when they will see a return on their investment. You may just need to give generalities about being acquired or going public. Failure to do so suggests an amateurish insensitivity to an investor's highest priority. The investor probably won't mention what's missing; you just won't be funded.

An elevator pitch is another key ingredient. This is a very short synopsis of your business plan, so named because it must be brief enough to be presented during an elevator ride. It should be no more than a sentence or two and give the basic idea of your business in memorable form. It's designed to build excitement and interest in your concept—to engage the listener enough to make her want to read your business plan. Skip the details and highlight your online education venture's potential benefits. Make it sound unique, but not unrealistic—perhaps comparing it to a business in another industry: "This is the McDonald's of online education ventures." Then explain why.

Show Me the e-Money

Not many of us have an angel investor hanging from the family tree or even in our circle of acquaintances. The solution is to widen the circle, actively networking and seizing every opportunity to find backers. You can also turn to the internet for help. Just typing the words "angel funding" or "venture capital" into a search engine like Google (www.google.com) or AltaVista (www.altavisa.com) will garner you a wealth of possibilities. Of course, as with most internet searches, the problem is sifting through the avalanche of responses you'll find. During one recent outing with Google, "angel funding" produced more than 150,000 results. "Venture capital" coughed up over 1.8 million. Most of those hits are duplicates, dead ends, articles where the words "angel" or "capital" appear, or even links to get-rich-quick schemers with a line in the water for the unwary.

Still, even finance pros use the internet. The good news is that angels and VCs are out there. They even have their own web pages. The National Venture Capital Association's (www.nvca.org) home page, for example, offers a directory of its 400-plus members. There are West Coast angel networks and East Coast angel networks, and everything in between. You're still left with a formidable job. But it's a start. And imagine how much better off you are than the entrepreneur of a decade ago who had to, what, look in the Yellow Pages under "Benefactor"?

Also check out the wealth of articles on this topic. *Entrepreneur* magazine (www.entrepreneur.com), for example, has an extensive archive of funding-oriented articles that include tips, suggestions, and contact information for many reliable sources.

Like most things in business, attracting funds is more art than science. It's a highly individualized, sometimes quixotic, pursuit that can't be reduced to a boilerplate. But it always benefits from a sprinkling of enthusiasm and even some healthy chutzpah.

The biggest drawback when seeking out angel investors or venture capitalists is that thousands of other soon-to-be or would-be entrepreneurs are doing the same thing. There is tremendous competition for those special investors. For this reason, starting small with a combination of a small business loan, some of your own personal savings, and perhaps a few small loans from those who know and love you (or at least believe in you) is a more practical approach. Also, don't forget that you can barter your way into many initial dealings for some things you need. Noncompetitive up-and-coming businesses often help each other out by striking deals, such as a couple of free computer desks and chair rentals for a free ad on your web site once it's up and running.

Real-World Rainmakers

In your search, one place you might consider checking out is a nearby college or university—particularly one with a business school that sponsors plan-writing competitions with seed money for prizes. "It's not the prize money but the contacts and exposure that make these get-togethers worthwhile," says Joseph Saari, co-founder of Precision Information in Madison, Wisconsin. His company develops software and other educational materials to teach adults about personal finance.

The $4,000 Saari won for third prize in a University of Wisconsin plan-writing competition didn't go far. In fact, Saari gave it all to MBA classmates who helped get his plan ready for competition. He came away with something far more valuable—a partner and mentor. Ed Harris, the retired founder of a successful Madison software company and a frequent judge in the University of Wisconsin competition, was so impressed by Saari's concept and by Saari himself that he approached the graduate student after the competition. The two agreed to co-found Precision Information.

"By far, the most valuable capital anyone contributes to a business is human capital," says Saari. "Having an experienced team involved and having them willing to work long hours is so much more valuable than having a pot of cash." And potential investors will look closely at your organizational chart and advisory board, notes Harris.

Perseverance Pays

How bad is the funding environment right now? Not bad enough to keep entrepreneurs down.

Stephen Shank started his online Capella University in Minneapolis under more difficult circumstances. It was 1993, when many people hadn't even heard of the internet; web connections were dominated by 14.4Kbps modems, and the dotcom boom hadn't yet happened. He was one of the very first to create such an institution. That made for an exciting start-up phase. Few could understand his business model, and even fewer believed it would succeed. "It wasn't easy to get anybody to provide outside financing to such a concept," says Shank.

Initially, his company was financed by himself and a small-scale venture capitalist who specialized in educational ventures. "The two of us literally bootstrapped this venture from 1993 until 1998, when the concept began to be more plausible to the outside sector," he says.

Network and Network Again

Few entrepreneurs bump into a rainmaker in business school or get a yes out of the first angel they pitch. Here's where persistent networking comes in.

Sarah Chapman and Devin Williams, co-founders of Spry Learning, are also graduates of business schools with business plan competitions. But they attracted angel financing the old-fashioned way, by wearing down shoe leather. While hammering out the special coursework needed and adjusting their business plan to meet the needs of the senior market, Chapman and Williams became regulars at state and national conventions devoted to gerontology and retirement communities. They began going up to the speakers at these venues (total strangers) and launching right into their elevator pitch.

"You just keep doing it until get your pitch down," says Williams. "The more people you talk to, the more concise your pitch becomes. You learn to get the point across quickly."

After many rejections and referrals, Chapman and Williams finally hooked up with angel investors who understood their sector and whose needs and time frame were compatible with Spry's marketing plan.

"This process can be frustrating and puzzling," says Williams. "Two investors look at the same business plan, and one will say, 'I'm concerned about this, but I feel great about that.' The other will have exactly the opposite reaction."

“It depends on their backgrounds and deals they’ve seen, and sometimes a lot of it has to do with personalities,” says Williams. “Sometimes you need an icebreaker—unrelated things you might have in common like playing tennis. But, at the end of the day, it behooves an entrepreneur to find someone who has a background in the things they are interested in and feels some of the same passion.”

Williams and Chapman raised a couple hundred thousand dollars in March 2000—not the best of times. Spry Learning reached the break-even point after its first year of operation.

Beware!

When it comes to pitching an idea and looking for investors at any level, you have to be “the answer person.” This means that you need to think through your plan so carefully that you are ready to answer any possible question that could be thrown your way. As soon as you are tongue tied and at a loss for words, you are through. Investors are expecting you to be very well-prepared and ready to answer the tough questions. So, before you pitch your ideas to anyone, practice, practice, practice . . . and have someone close to you play devil’s advocate. However, very long-winded answers may also give the impression that you are talking until you come up with something. Therefore, be ready with one to three sentences to answer anything they could possibly throw at you.

Some keys to networking include:

- *Finding some common ground.* This may be easier at a convention or conference where you are probably with like-minded people.
- *Know when to appraoch and when to back off.* Timing is very important. If your would-be investor is with family, in a meeting, in a tanning booth, or anyplace else where you don’t belong, leave him or her alone. Look for opportune times where he or she is waiting (not checking his or her watch in a panic), at the break during a seminar or lecture, or at a business engagement and not otherwise engaged in conversation. Be selective when you approach someone.
- *Listen.* Far too many people make the mistake of doing all the talking and/or not listening to a word the other party has to say.
- *Have your business card handy.* Be ready to cut the conversation short when the other person’s ride, business associate, husband/wife, or whomever shows up.
- *Leave with a polite handshake.* Don’t kiss, no high fives . . . a simple handshake.
- *Don’t hand out the business plan.* Be ready to send the business plan, but not ready to run around handing it out to everyone—that creates the appearance of over-eagerness, which is a short step away from appearing desperate.

Stretching Exercises

How did Spry Learning turn so little into so much? In very much the same way cited by Precision Information, eLearning, and other successful entrepreneurs: doing more with less. Spry runs a ten-person company in modest office space, and relies on activities coordinators employed by retirement communities to bring its curricula to seniors.

Smart Tip

Tip...

Don't forget to work through professional associations (industry, software, or educational) where you can network your way toward crucial early investments.

"Not having a lot of overhead lets you get to break-even quickly before running out of money," explains Williams. "You don't want to be in that position where you need something, and you have to get it. The worse time to raise money is when you need it."

The Shoestring Stage

Purse strings loosen up considerably once you can prove that your idea works and generates a revenue stream. Getting an online learning business started on a small budget is not impossible. The trick is doing something different and/or serving a largely untapped market. Students will pay for interesting courses by interesting people as long as you are giving them quality content for their dollar. Yes, more money enables you to utilize more elaborate technologies and present course information in more intriguing ways, but the key is selling knowledge, creativity, and innovation. Remember, as mentioned at the start of the chapter, methods of learning go back thousands of years. It's not about the computers and technology you use. These are simply your means of reaching the audience. Companies that have overextended themselves on the technical end (and this is not exclusive to online learning) have found out the hard way that content is the key . . . or in their cases, should have been the key.

Beware!

Don't co-mingle your business and personal funds. Yes, the temptation is great and many startups are funded with home equity loans and personal credit cards. But tax troubles lie in wait for those who process receivables through personal accounts. It's a red flag for the IRS, which may even disallow some business deductions on that basis.

Pricing Your Courses

Part of your business plan, and an important aspect of piquing the interest of potential investors, is what you will charge for courses.

Making a Statement

One of the trickier elements of any business plan is creating the necessary financial statements with three- or five-year revenue projections. Given the uncertainties of business, sales projections are speculative even for established businesses. They're especially challenging to predict before you've really started to make money.

"Venture funders understand this," says Synnovation chief executive Ed Harris. But this is a crucial exercise. While your actual experience will differ, budgets and sales projections do need to be grounded as much as possible in reality.

"Prospective investors are likely to look most closely at your first-year projections," says Harris. He wants to see not too much but not too little allocated for research and development—ideally, 10 to 12 percent. Sales and marketing should account for another 10 to 25 percent, depending on the type of company and its stage of development. Keep a close eye on whether or not you are looking to hire too many people. In the heyday of the internet, companies were hiring left and right. Pretty soon dotcomers were looking around a crowded office wondering what half the people working there were actually doing. In some cases, those people were also wondering why they were hired. Make sure you plan to utilize your employees to the fullest and are not padding the payroll before you even start. Two-, three-, and five-member teams have done great things. So, if you don't NEED a dozen people, don't spend money on hiring a dozen people.

Take your time and work with your accountant or financial advisor when making your projections.

Investors want to know that you have a plan for making a profit from all of your hard work, and that your plan is grounded in reality. The cost per student per course is, therefore, very important and varies widely depending on the context in which you are selling your product. Are you selling a highly in-demand IT certification course? Masters degree courses for a diploma? French language courses to seniors? The desire or need for a course, the audience to which you are selling the course, and the current market dictate how much you can charge per course.

Testing aside, many online courses can run as little as two to three hours or as long as 24 hours' worth of intermittent asynchronous coursework. But the typical course is between six and eight hours. Prices are all over the map—from $30 to $400 or even $600. They generally reflect market demand and the potential economic value to come from certification in that topic. In contrast, classroom-based IT courses can run as high as $2,800 a week. And that usually doesn't count certification exams or the boot camps you might attend to practice for those exams.

It also makes a difference who is offering them and where. For example, Oracle offered attendees of OracleWorld a series of certification exams for $50 each. The exams normally would have cost more than $100 through Oracle University.

Determining pricing for your courses should start with a simple internet search of what the competition is doing. Then comes the hard part—deciding whether you are looking for high margins or rapid market penetration, and calculating how well you can communicate your unique added value to the marketplace.

Smart Tip

While they are not angels or investors, you can benefit from checking out SCORE, a nationwide organization that features retired executive who serve as mentors and advisors to businesses. Billed as "Counselors to America's small businesses," SCORE can provide you with someone to provide business knowledge and ideas starting during the crucial planning phase before you begin to seek funding.

As *Certification* magazine points out, IT pros pay for all or some of their training courses a little more than half the time, with employers picking up the other tabs. "They are making a very real investment, so it is natural that with such an investment, these professionals expect more than a feel-good result from their certifications—they expect an economic return." Therefore, you can charge more money for IT courses.

According to *Certification* magazine's research on certifications (both in-classroom and online), the return on the investment is easily identified. Including travel and materials, as well as fees, the average certification costs $1,934. Of this total amount, $338 is spent on materials. On average, more than half (53 percent) of those certified report they got a raise within the first year of attaining their primary certification, and 37 percent received a promotion.

The situation with post-graduate degrees is similar, with students benefiting financially from the courses. However, the market for nondegree courses, while still very large, is one in which you will need to look more closely at competing online schools. For example, most of the courses from CourseBridge (from three to seven lessons) run between $69 and $99. Since these are noncredit courses for personal growth and enjoyment, these are numbers that have proven to be cost effective. You will need to build your own cost-effective numbers based on how much it takes to present a course and pay an instructor, how much marketing you need to do to draw each student, and how much profit margin you are looking for. Take your time and punch a lot of numbers when planning your course fees. And, have them ready when you pitch your business to investors.

13

Spreading the Word

This chapter presents an overview of the ways successful online education entrepreneurs employ advertising and marketing, including public relations. Because marketing dollars are wasted unless you can keep customers, we also take a look at customer service.

The marketing methods recommended are not mutually exclusive. None is necessarily best for you. Over time, you will figure out which combination of marketing, promotion, advertising, and/or public relations translates into getting and maintaining customers for your business. The key is to develop your plan as quickly and cheaply as possible.

It's an Ad, Ad, Ad World

The web is the watershed development for online learning. We all recognize the extent of the opportunity. But recent years have taught us in the most memorable way possible that few companies have yet figured out how to exploit it.

The fundamental principles of good marketing in the virtual world are similar to those in the real world, principles long established and successfully time tested. Those who have succeeded have generally followed those principles, mixing viral or other New Economy forms of marketing with more traditional modes of marketing, such as cold calling or direct mail. Still, the internet is a new medium, offering its own unique set of advertising and other marketing opportunities and challenges compared to print, radio, or television.

Company size and geography are no longer as important as they were. web-based or web-oriented businesses can reach out to customers around the world—in theory at least, although that can be very expensive, and the whole world may not be your "target market." On the internet, your site is just one of millions. You must figure out inexpensive ways to gather potential customers.

Some online educational businesses, such as resellers or service firms working with corporate clients, need a presence in their geographical location. Selecting the right advertising vehicle is still tough—as it is for any brick-and-mortar business—but you have a more manageable number of newspapers, specialized publications, radio and TV stations, and mailers from which to choose. But which, if any, bring students in the door? Advertising is expensive, and start-ups don't have a surplus of funds.

Mark Carey, chief executive of reseller MySoftwareHelper, alternately advertised on local radio and in local computer newspapers and law journals. These did not prove effective. "We tracked the calls from print ads through our web site, and I don't think I got one bit of business out of all that radio and print advertising," says Carey. "I got a couple of calls, but not one close. The ads were creative, they were flashy, they were cute. But they just didn't pay off."

Name a target market, and you'll find that your friendly local ad sales representative has no trouble at all demonstrating statistically that his or her media outlet reaches those individuals. But the proper use of advertising takes long, hard research and a very carefully planned and executed advertising campaign. Flying by the seat of

Beware!

Web banner ads are often sold by cost-per-thousand (CPM), that is, how many times the page is viewed. But views alone aren't that fruitful. You care more about how many people actually click on your ad, the click-through rate. You care most, of course, about those who actually buy. Be sure to analyze traffic on your web site to see what's working.

your pants and using trial and error can run your advertising budget down to zero before you find the right medium for your business. Additionally, throwing up a single ad won't do it. You must try not just once but over a decent period of time. Advertising is about persistence, and recognition by the consumer. People familiarize themselves with products and services they hear or read about on a regular basis, not just one time. You pay based on cost-per-thousand impressions (CPM), but people rarely buy the first time they see an ad. Usually, they must see your message many times before they get a sense of your permanence and the impulse to buy is translated into action. You also stand a better chance of reaching someone at that moment when they may be considering taking a course if you become the online school that first pops into their heads. Therefore, persistence builds name familiarity.

"If you're going to advertise, you need pretty deep pockets to pound away month after month after month," says Carey, "and most small businesses can't afford that." Assuming you have found the right venue for your audience, getting the response you want depends on a number of other factors—your message, the creative quality of your ad, the time of day or even the season it is delivered, and even outside events.

Being creative helps, but sometimes, you just can't be creative enough. Think of Super Bowl TV ads—some people find them as entertaining as the game itself, but only rarely does lightning strike so that they pay off. Typically, these are major companies with excessively deep pockets such as Coke, FedEx, or major movie studios, that can use that ad for months after that springboard debut on the Super Bowl.

In the Virtual World

As difficult as it is to craft a good local advertising campaign, it's even tougher to get a good return on ads if, say, yours is an IT certification business or online university whose students may come from all over the country. Yes, the University of Phoenix (www.phoenix.edu) spends massive amounts of money on their ads for online courses. But a start-up can't enjoy that option.

The internet is inherently global in focus. Even though a banner ad, pop-up, or other web advertising technique may seem to have a low CPM compared to other venues, they reach vast numbers of people you don't care about. Therefore, you might opt for less expensive ads on smaller, more targeted sites. For example, an IT training certification course advertised on a less "mass audience" site where IT professionals may be found more often can prove much more cost effective. Likewise, ads in trade journals can help and are more affordable than ads in national popular publications read by more people, most of whom are not your audience.

Tip...

Smart Tip

Run traffic analysis software on your web site so that you can keep tabs on what type of visitors you get, which pages they look at, which links or offers they respond to, how long they spend on the site, where they come from, where they go, and other important statistics.

Zeroing In: Yahoo! Yes, but the Main Page, No

Just as major television stations with national audiences also sell local advertising spots in each market (for much less money), you can also zero in on a targeted page within a larger web site. For example, unless your target audience is nearly universal, buying a basic ad on a main page on a site like Yahoo! is not cost-effective. Yahoo! will be only too happy to place the ad. It's a high-traffic site that probably does a good job for consumer product or lifestyle companies. But its top pages will scoop up a lot of viewers who don't match up with your market. You'll be casting your net too wide, spending money on many people who won't be able to take advantage of your services by virtue of geography or interest.

Instead, you want to pick a specific page on Yahoo!—say, the directory page for the "Distance Learning/Computers" page or the page that comes up when you search on "IT certification." Another option if you're an online university or IT training company might be to advertise on education portals like Colleges.com (www.colleges.com) or eLearners.com (www.elearners.com). If you are targeting knowledge workers, try a job board such as Monster.com (www.monster.com). Even here, you may still be casting your net too widely.

As for web search engines, it may be very effective to pay for premium placement on the web's major search engines like Google, AltaVista, AllTheWeb.com, Inktomi, and Teoma. Of course, this is costly ($10,000 or more per month on Google) and only effective if you have a wide range of courses to meet the many possible hits. Basically, you pay to be in the first few listings that come up with searches on different keywords. This is the only type of advertising Mark Carey of MySoftwareHelper uses now, and he says that it provides good results. Some search engines focus on particular topics or communities.

Each engine operates a little differently, but Google is the most popular search engine. A site page on Google (www.google.com/ads/overview.html) will tell you everything you need to know about this kind of advertising.

You also want to learn about web optimization, which means finding ways to boost your site up to the first few pages on internet search engines. This involves keywords and keyword phrases, placement and positioning of keywords, META tags, titles and title tags, and much more. You can find information on how to optimize your site at web sites such as www.web-source.net/webpage_optimizing.htm or by searching online for search engine optimization. One of the hottest businesses today is search optimization. Once you've found someone to help you optimize your own site, you might consider hiring that person to teach an optimization course for your business.

> Tip...
>
> **Smart Tip**
>
> If you want to place a banner ad on a web site, you'll be quoted a CPM rate or cost per 1,000 visits. Here's how to calculate how much it costs you to attract each visitor to your site with your ad. With 100,000 visits and a click-through rate of 0.4 per 1,000 visits, you get 40 visits. If your CPM is $2, the ad costs $200, so each visit costs $5.

Seasoning

Web advertising and marketing don't easily reduce to broad generalizations. They need to be seasoned with a little common sense. In the case of IT certification, the number-one place that professionals go to find online learning providers is the equipment vendor's web site, according to Apex InfoTech in Irvine, California. Apex gets most of its business from the Microsoft web site and doesn't even pay for most of those referrals. It's just on a list of authorized trainers that Microsoft provides for web visitors.

Don't forget that if your ads do start to pay off, you must be thoroughly prepared to respond quickly and effectively, whether that means taking questions and orders over the phone or kicking product delivery over your web site. Have your system(s) in place before you advertise for taking all types of registration.

Telling the PR Story

There are other ways to get your message out, including public relations. Here the goal is to get your company's name in the media without having to pay for it. For that reason, it is sometimes referred to as "free advertising." But while you don't pay directly for the coverage, PR is neither free nor easy to come by.

PR specialists try to generate interest among journalists, editors, and producers on your behalf by presenting them with newsworthy information that is relevant to each specific publication, and you'll pay them for the hours they spend doing it. You may be surprised at their low rate of success. It isn't a reflection on the PR folk necessarily, but rather the difficulty of the task. The problem is that editors and producers, who are in the decision-making process of what goes into print, on a web site, or on the air, are often besieged by press releases pitching all sorts of stories. Getting yours to stand out isn't even half the battle . . . getting it read at all, is the first major hurdle. For that reason, the creativity and ingenuity of a good publicist is almost as important as his or her contact list. Major PR firms charge corporate clients thousands of dollars every month via retainers to "blitz the market." The reality, of course, is that many PR pros will tell you (off the record) that they spend far less time then they should on each of too many major accounts. They know that the market is saturated and, quite frankly, aren't always sure where to send PR material to get it seen or read.

Therefore, a small business needs a more personalized, local PR person or agency, where it's possible to track what *is* actually being done on your behalf. During start-up, you can hire a well-connected individual freelance PR person for about $60 to $100 per hour. A one-person show won't necessarily have all the resources of a full-fledged PR firm—maybe not all of the marketing savvy and staffers ready to launch a major campaign—but you don't need all of that to get started. You can find these people through your extensive ongoing business networking. Get samples of their work and check out their references. Make sure they are well-connected, since you are paying largely for their contact lists.

You also can do your own PR. The founders of Spry Learning combine market research with good PR by becoming experts on seniors' training at as many trade shows and conferences as they have time for. Mark Carey of MySoftwareHelper also makes numerous presentations and sometimes appears on local radio or public TV stations as an educational expert. Other chief executives stay in touch with key media contacts by phone or e-mail; many even give "virtual press tours" online.

Often you can get started with some ideas yourself and then bring in a PR pro (as a freelancer) to polish the press release and do placement. The key is having an angle that makes your story unique. For Spry, it was being the first to create an online learning center specifically designed for adults. For you, it may be a unique means of delivering a course, courses taught by well-known individuals who

Dollar Stretcher

You may be able to go cheaper by hiring a PR agency for individual projects, as opposed to the monthly retainer that they prefer. You may have to shop around a little, but the agency must account for each hour it bills.

have not taught before, or courses that are either unique or tie into something that is in the news.

You can easily find sample press releases and learn to write them yourself. A quality press release grabs the attention of the reader in a headline, talks about the key news or information in the first paragraph and expands with some details in the second. The third paragraph is usually a boilerplate paragraph explaining your business in general, with contact information. Short, to the point, newsworthy, and without extraneous information—those are the keys to a good press release. Provide the who, what, where, why, and when of the story in a succinct, interesting manner. Web sites like PRWeb Direct (www.prwebdirect.com/pressreleasetips.php) or xpresspress.com (www.xpress press.com/PRnotes.html), among others, have the how-to's of press release writing plus samples.

On the plus side, high-tech media are plentiful, and the general business press is very amenable to tech stories (often more so than to education stories per se). Also, newspapers, news-oriented magazines, and the electronic media with high frequencies (such as dailies) and plenty of space to fill may be easier to get into.

Even so, your PR representative will need a little luck and fortuitous timing. Public relations typically requires establishing and building relationships on your behalf to establish media contacts, put your name out in front of the media, and keep it there so that when a story on a related topic comes up, assignment editors and journalists think of you.

If you do get the press to write favorably about you, however, it can be more beneficial than a dozen ads. Since this is a recommendation of sorts from an independent third party, it usually carries considerably more value with the audience than an ad. Having a major magazine devote a page to the efficacy of your training would be thousands of times more beneficial than a dozen ads.

PR is about overcoming inertia. A story in *Time* magazine would, in all likelihood, be the first pickle out of the jar for you. Your PR representative would use it as a testimonial to get attention from other media. Spry Learning in Portland, Oregon, was lucky enough to get an article on its seniors training early on in the *Los Angeles Times*. It resulted in numerous other press contacts and profiles on the company, which it uses them as testimonials on its web site. The idea here is to use whatever good press you get to try to start a snowball effect, generating more attention as you go.

Tip...

Smart Tip

If you do computer training, join a computer user group or two and give free presentations at meetings. These groups are all over America and a great way to heighten your profile and establish your expertise. In major urban centers, you can probably find a user or other affinity group that closely matches the demographics of your target audience.

This process can work in reverse, too: Reporters on big publications may follow up on a story they spot in more specialized publications. It might just be a simple press release announcing your existence or a backgrounder on your company. It might be one of those ongoing campaigns to keep putting your name out in front of the media.

Online Newsletters

One of the mistakes many businesses make when doing marketing and public relations is constantly going after new customers. In reality, most businesses have an 80–20 rate of business, meaning 80 percent of their business is from return customers and 20 percent from newcomers. It is also much less expensive to keep a customer coming back than to reach out to find and cultivate new ones. With that in mind, you need to have a marketing campaign geared toward your current customers, letting them know what is going on with your business. Fliers, handouts, and signage works well for brick-and-mortar businesses. However, since you are operating in the cyber world, you need to utilize cyber means of staying in touch with your customers. This can include e-mails to people who have agreed to receive e-mails from you (not spam). However, e-mails get boring if they are only promotional, and people tend to delete them unless they are thinking of taking a course at that very minute. Therefore, an online newsletter can be a marvelous way of self-promoting, one that is attention grabbing, cost effective, and fairly easy to put together.

There are a few key things to remember when putting together an e-mail newsletter. First, you want to send it only to people who have opted in to receive it. Therefore, opting in should be an option on your web site and in all means of marketing. You do not want to send to people off of purchased lists for two reasons. First, it is likely that the people on the list have not granted permission to send to them, which makes your e-mail spam and sends your reputation and credibility down the drain with those people receiving (and deleting) it. Secondly, most often the lists are old and many of the contacts—web addresses, or other means of contact—are dated.

It is important to provide content in a newsletter. Content can come in the form of two or three paragraphs about something related to what you offer. If, for example, you offer writing classes, then perhaps an article about five great new places to get nonfiction articles published. Perhaps you are marketing IT courses. Then, an article on a new trend in technology might suffice. Relate the article to your courses, but do not make it read as an advertisement—make it content. The goal is to have people want to read your newsletter. They won't do this if every time it's just a bunch of ads. Just as we watch television shows and read magazines for content and accept the ads, your audience will accept your promotions and ads (around the content) as long as they are getting some information that proves to be useful, entertaining, educational, or meets some need. Content draws the reader's attention. The promotions all around the content—for your courses—is where you should advertise.

You also want to have a means of forwarding an article (with the accompanying ad) to a friend, which helps you spread the word virally. It helps if you can throw in a good tip for programmers, a great quote, funny anecdote, a tasteful joke, or even a recipe (if you're teaching culinary classes). You can prompt people to send such tidbits to a friend, again with your promotion always attached. There are certain items, including e-cards, that people love to forward to others. Word-of-mouth advertising has proven very successful, and it costs you nothing. Find a means by which to inspire your newsletter readers to "forward to a friend" or talk your newsletter up at the water cooler. Every target market group, be it teachers, IT professionals, or auto mechanics, enjoys trivia tidbits or a funny anecdote that relates to their business.

Make sure your newsletter is concise—people will scroll down a little bit, but not forever—content should be front and center when they click on the newsletter.

It's important to make sure your newsletter has a professional look to it, including proper spelling and grammar. Limit the bells and whistles because you don't want to risk slow downloads that result in your reader getting bored and deleting it. You also need to make your newsletter content of interest to THEM. Don't include inside information, such as what your business partner did over the holidays; they don't care. Far too many newsletters lose their audience due to self-indulgence.

Finally, keep them coming bi-weekly or monthly. If the response is very favorable, perhaps weekly, but that takes more commitment on your part. It means finding and stockpiling story ideas. You should develop a template early on through some trial and error system, allowing you to paste in the content and the ads (for your courses) with ease.

If you accept outside advertising to support the cost of the newsletter, make sure ads from other businesses do not detract from *your* newsletter. Often a banner ad for another company on top of a newsletter indicates to readers that it's the newsletter of that company.

A Welcome Site for Customers

Before we leave the topic of advertising and public relations, let's talk again about your best source of marketing—your own web site. It's both an advertising and a PR vehicle. As we know, a web site is your own personal billboard alongside the information superhighway. Granted, it's a highway broader than the Amazon River and every inch of space on either side is crowded with similar billboards. But it costs you so little to put up a basic billboard, and the display advertising aspect is only the start of its usefulness.

Your site will be, in a sense, the central clearinghouse for all your marketing efforts, a cheap way to distribute information to potential customers and the most convenient place for them to connect with you.

You'll include your URL on your business cards, stationery, marketing material, packaging labels, merchandising giveaways, and in any ads you place elsewhere. Your URL will usually become more important than your street address and telephone number since you are, after all, running an online business.

Smart Tip

Want a good web site model? Nielsen/NetRatings (www.nielsen-netratings.com) measures the top 25 web sites each week. The sites can afford the best and brightest web page designers and marketers to work on them. You can get good design hints and traffic-building ideas from them.

Most good dotcom domain names are taken. But even if you do manage to snag a URL in the ".com" domain, you also should make sure that yours is the site on which web surfers are most likely to land by also registering your URL in the more recently opened dot.biz and dot.us domains. Depending on the nature of your business, you may even fit in the dot.edu or dot.pro domains. It's worth a try at the very least. Each registration will cost $25 to $50 a year—pretty cost-effective even if you only get one customer out of it.

You might be able to pay for that cost by becoming an associate of other web sites—that is, by providing them with referrals that turn into business for them.

Likewise, you'll want to get a link to your site in the link lists of as many related sites as you can. LearnKey gets 100,000 visitors a month to its site (www.learnkey.com). Get in the newsletters of related sites—either through advertising or PR (being an education expert). You may even want to advertise on a site like LearnKey.

Remember to keep an eye on your site to make sure it's up and running effectively, and always respond quickly (within 24 hours) to any e-mail or other messages it generates.

Getting Sticky

In addition to finding a way to rise above the clamor and clutter of the internet, you want to make the most of the visitors who do land on your site. Good graphics and an easily navigable site are important, of course. But they are really just the ante in the game. They aren't really what holds people or gets them to buy once they land on your site. Demos of your courses will help—people want to check out the product, and the more time they spend with you, the more likely they are to make a connection.

You want to have a "sticky" web site. Stickiness refers to techniques or features that hold people on your site, get them to navigate around and investigate more deeply,

Beware!

If you plan to use an e-mail newsletter to keep new and current students coming back to your site, remember to make sure that it's the opt-in variety. You can send them an invitation, but don't distribute marketing materials to just any e-mail list. People's patience for spam is already sorely tested, and you run the risk of battles with the FCC if you are caught as a spammer. Even worse, you can lose credibility.

and keep them coming back. They don't necessarily come back every time to buy something. However, each time they return to your site, they are exposed to what you offer. The longer and more often they are exposed, the more likely they are to spend money.

Making your web site "sticky" may mean giving away something for free in hopes of selling something else. You might do it by offering a series of free short courses, which serve the purpose of introducing students to your site. As they continually revisit your site to see what you are giving way, you can promote the fee-based courses as well.

Another way to maximize the business you get from each customer is with an online incentive or loyalty program, much like the loyalty programs of supermarkets and airlines. You set up an array of awards for behaviors you want to encourage in your site visitors. There are many ways to approach it; a very common one is to set up a frequent buyer/visitor rewards program that doles out points that eventually earn visitors discounts or prizes—maybe from your site, often from the sites of your partners. Assign points when customers buy products, of course, but also by amount. They can get points when they register online, fill out a market survey, or refer a friend who registers (which is often referred to as viral marketing). You also can dole out points for various holiday promotions. It's a simple enough program to set up inhouse. But you can also outsource your program to a company that offers turnkey points programs such as MyPoints.com (www.mypoints.com).

You can also draw people back to your web site by updating it with pertinent information and even inexpensive web seminars that touch upon current events and relate to courses you offer. You need to keep the web site fresh. Offering chat rooms or a bulletin board can also have people coming back to discuss pertinent issues with each other, also while seeing your promotions for related courses.

Show Your Stuff

Depending on your type of online education business, shows may be an excellent means of drawing students. Trade shows (local, regional, and national), conferences, seminars, professional association meetings, and other meetings all let you get your name and face out in front of the public. As with everything else, only certain shows and conferences will work for you. An online learning trade show may be informative, but if dominated by people just like you, it may or may not generate customers.

Selection isn't always obvious. Mark Carey of MySoftwareHelper has had his best marketing success at the Seattle I-Tech show, a local version of a nationwide show series. But Carey also has enjoyed success selling to Indian tribal councils. Spry Learning, which targets seniors, attends the annual conferences for the Assisted Living Federation of America and the American Association for Homes and Services for the Aging, as well as the affiliated

Tip...

Smart Tip

Learn the ins and outs of trade show exhibiting at The TradeShow Coach (www.TheTradeShowCoach.com). This web site includes articles, books, tapes, workshops, and free weekly e-mail tips.

Spread Your Merchandise

Try a marketing method that can be employed relatively cheaply in both the real and virtual worlds: merchandising. Merchandising is something you do to entice new students, hold onto current students, or get them to buy up without cutting your prices or devaluing your brand.

It can be used in conjunction with both your advertising and PR, as well as your effort to make your web site sticky. To take one rather prosaic example, you could offer a virtual gift certificate on your web page for visitors who bring you a successful referral. The gift could be an introductory course or courseware or a prize you've worked out with another site—say, $10 worth of merchandise on an electronics web site.

At the very least, you're likely to capture marketing information on both the referrer and referee through your merchandising efforts. You can make the gift certificate a part of your advertising and PR materials. It might put an immediacy to your ad that gets people moving. You can also use it to build traffic at your trade show booth.

Here again, having a web page saves you money over traditional real-world merchandising methods (not that they don't also have merit). Your virtual gift certificate is better than a paper certificate because there are no printing or distribution costs involved. You can change your materials in five minutes in response to the action without incurring printing costs all over again. A classic example: The Bay Area's Le Boulangerie bakery chain offered instant online coupons for a pastry to those who logged onto the web using its wireless LAN hotspots.

state conferences and senior housing conferences for governmental organizations. "With conferences, you have a concentration of hundreds or thousands of people—experts in the industry," explains Spry co-founder Devin Williams. "You can make presentations of your own, listen to speakers, and talk to people in the industry. It's a good way to get both information and attention." Even when they don't exhibit, MySoftwareHelper and Spry make trade shows pay off by presenting in the seminars.

Running a booth like LearnKey's at a conference can be expensive. You can easily spend between $10,000 and $50,000 for a high-profile trade show appearance—not just for space, but for staffing and merchandising materials, and perhaps a reception or two. There are creative firms that specialize in creating effective trade show displays and events, and they can cost you thousands of dollars themselves. But there are cheaper ways to go, too, starting with the size and design of your booth and the number of people who attend from your company.

Not every square foot of trade show floor space costs the same. Giant LearnKey often commands a good deal of booth space at the shows it attends. MySoftwareHelper and Spry maintain a lesser profile farther out toward the edges of the trade show floor. There's also space available in smaller booths along the show floor perimeter—the cheap seats. Devin Williams figures that a booth for two days costs between $800 and $1,800. It costs Spry around $5,000 to go to national shows, but it often can get by for under $2,000 at smaller, regional shows.

Both the leads and the notoriety generated can take some time to pay off. "You can recoup that, but it doesn't necessarily happen the first year you do it," says Williams. "It's very good exposure—people start thinking about it and when they start talking about it, your name comes up, and people start to refer to you."

Word-of-Mouth

Whatever your business, you need excellent customer service, which generates favorable word of mouth. So, you can think of word-of-mouth marketing and customer service as two sides of the same coin.

Good reputations don't happen overnight and can't be bought with ads and press releases. Yes, other marketing efforts start the process, but good reputations can be sustained only by delivering on a promise.

When you come recommended, the sale is almost a done deal. As you start building up a customer base, you'll want to make sure that every customer's experience with you and your employees is favorable. That usually means going above and beyond the call to make sure that the customer has a good experience.

Part of customer service is customer relationship management, which means actively nurturing the relationship you have with each customer—cross-selling, if you can. Always give customers more than they can get from your competition. To do this, study their preferences and anticipate their needs. You never know when some action on your part will lead to an unanticipated sale.

Customer service is considered a cost center by most large companies, who seem more willing to invest in elaborate call centers and technology than in individuals who can really help. A start-up that handles service more personally can generate pleasant memories for customers and draw them back again.

Good customer service is easy to talk about, easy to put in your press releases, but harder to fulfill. It means responding to problems, concerns, and even questions quickly and in a manner that is helpful. If you have a staff, it means training everyone to do the same. Your goal is to maintain a strong relationship with each customer. This can result in your business standing out and generating positive word of mouth by providing quality customer service.

14

Failure and Success

This chapter discusses the elements of success for entrepreneurial ventures. It also provides insights that help in getting your online education learning business off the ground. Finally, we share the hard-won wisdom of several of the entrepreneurs whom we interviewed for this book and just a few of the ways they gained small victories that add up to long-term success.

Rocky Road

Economic events at the start of this decade are just the kind of lemons from which entrepreneurs have always made lemonade. If we hop back a couple of decades, we find a very similar set of economic circumstances—actually, a much more onerous set of conditions. But it was from double-digit inflation, double-digit interest rates, and tight capital that the latest entrepreneurial revolution emerged.

The intervening 20-plus years created a bumper crop of entrepreneurs. There were years of nearly unbroken progress with vast increases in American wealth, leapfrogging productivity improvements, the taming of consumer inflation, and the lowering of interest rates to the point where capital is readily available to U.S. businesses and consumers.

GEMS of Wisdom

The Global Entrepreneurship Monitor (GEM), funded by the Ewing Marion Kauffman Foundation, studies entrepreneurship and economic growth in 37 countries and identifies entrepreneurs as adults aged 18 to 64 involved in the start-up process or engaged as the owner/manager of a business less than 3½ years old.

Here are some findings from ongoing entrepreneurial research, with some surprises:

- More Americans are trying to create new companies than new marriages or babies.
- Despite strides made by female entrepreneurs, men are still about twice as likely to start new ventures as women.
- Individuals aged 25 to 44 are the most active age group of entrepreneurs.
- African-American men and women are about 50 percent more likely to start a business than Caucasian men and women, and those rates rise sharply with education levels.
- Rates of entrepreneurship rise significantly with levels of education, especially among minorities. Black and Hispanic men with post-graduate experience are at least twice as likely to be involved in a start-up than white men with similar education.
- Most entrepreneurs work in teams of about two people, but about 40 percent work alone.

As important as its activities may be, government doesn't create wealth. It doesn't come up with new ideas. It doesn't invent new, more efficient manufacturing, service, or managerial processes. It doesn't open factories or invest in product research. Government actions do not move the needle on the national productivity scale, which is the source of the new wealth that permits the creation of new jobs. The American government just lays the groundwork for others to do that.

Those that do move the needle are typically relatively young, relatively small companies. That's where the most innovation takes place. That's where most jobs and new wealth are created each year.

So, here we are and there you are, without the advantages of a cozy relationship with a regulatory agency, or a golden parachute, or a diversified product line and market dominance. You have to do things the hard way—from scratch. You have seemingly insurmountable obstacles and many long workdays in front of you. You need to play for real money in a game where the rules are always changing.

Yes, You Can

You can succeed anyway, like millions of entrepreneurs before you. That's not to minimize your individual challenges. You can't know in advance what they will be, what the right answer to them will be, or whether they will turn out to be opportunities in disguise. But success never travels alone. It's always accompanied by challenges, with new ones springing out of your solution to old ones. No one ever succeeded without them. But you can do it.

"When I started the company two years ago, I knew nothing about e-learning, had no contacts, and had no clue where to start," recalls Mark Carey of MySoft wareHelper. Actually, the slope was steeper than that for Carey. About the time that he decided he was tired of all the travel involved in being national sales manager for a large drug company, Carey's wife died, leaving him with their two little girls. In addition, there were legal complications that tied up all the family's assets—from insurance policies and mortgages right down to Carey's car registration and line of credit. A career change is a challenging period in just about anyone's life. But we can only guess at the additional emotional turmoil and complications involved in such a loss.

Eventually, Carey worked out the family finances and scraped together enough money to do the research and development for his business. He managed to interest an angel investor in his venture and was counting on that individual to provide the $250,000 needed to launch MySoftwareHelper. But the day Carey was to sign the contract to have his web site developed, the angel backed out. "I thought, 'I've done all this work and I'll be damned if I am going to let this die,'" Carey recalls. He cashed in his stock options from his previous job, found a cheaper web developer and ad agency, and pushed on.

When Carey first started calling on companies to sell online learning courseware, many were already locked into multiyear contracts with competing courseware companies who had broad but not complete lines. So he started his relationship with many companies by selling a single course that the other courseware providers didn't offer. Then, through diligent client service, he has convinced companies to convert to his courses. "Find a niche that your competitor isn't filling and go after that part of the business," advises Carey. "Find something customers need, and start building trust in your product line."

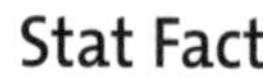

Stat Fact

About 286 million of the world's people, or 12 percent of the labor force in the 37 most industrialized nations, are involved in new business formation, according to the Ewing Marion Kauffman Foundation.

MySoftwareHelper is hugely successful. Asked why he chose online learning when he had no previous experience in education, Carey responds: "Why should that stop anybody? If you have an idea and know how to market yourself, it doesn't matter about your experience."

Don't Quit Until You Hit

New businesses require tremendous upfront effort without immediate return. You must develop your market, often with many early disappointments. Many have followed the "Build It and They Will Come" approach and found that customers didn't come. Many more quit before the customers discovered them. You'll need enough money to see you through. And you very well may need one or more mid-course corrections.

Carey never completes installation of a new corporate online learning system without asking the customer for contact information of other people in other departments or companies. He then calls on them, confident that the name he drops will give him a good recommendation. "I use testimonials to sell (to) more companies from the web site. But if I sell (to) a law firm, I call others and say, 'I just sold this course to so-and-so, and I understand that you may have a need for the same training. Would you be interested in sitting down and chatting?'"

Of course, the person making the original recommendation should be entirely happy with your offering. If the new sales prospect calls to check, you need a glowing recommendation.

First-Mover Advantage

Stephen Shank's biggest challenge when he set out to start his online university in Minneapolis in 1993 was that it was 1993. The internet, as we know and love it today, did not exist. The idea of a university online was, therefore, unproven. Shank's second challenge was to get the accreditation necessary for regulatory approval from the state licensing agency and federal government. At the time, both were very skeptical of the concept of online learning; it was a radical idea for most people. Fortunately, early pioneers like Shank blazed a trail so that it became easier for later entrepreneurs.

OK, so it's far too late for you to be the first online university. But online education is still far from mature. There is some way to innovate in your market. There is something your customers need that isn't being provided by others. Your mission is to evaluate what is out there and set your sights on providing something new and different, which, as was mentioned earlier, may be a new way of delivering educational materials or providing courses to a new demographic audience, as Spry did.

Tip...

Smart Tip

It requires discipline, but if you're sure you'll pay off the balance every month, you can enhance your cash flow by paying all suppliers with a credit card. You get the 28 days of float from the card company and tons of frequent flier miles that can offset business travel expenses. In addition, you can boost your business credit rating—as long as you don't fall behind. This will help you when you take on future tasks, such as moving into a larger space or upgrading some of your computer technology and doing so by using a business loan. In fact, the more short-term business loans you take out and pay off immediately, the better your credit will be when you need a larger loan for a bigger need.

Getting Feedback

If you don't seek out feedback, you'll never know what students, instructors, and clients think of your efforts. It is imperative for the success of any business to keep tabs on how they are perceived in the business community, in their own industry, and in the media. If you proceed in a vacuum, you may be meandering along a road to nowhere.

Feedback will allow you to gauge how you are doing. Just as when Coke or Pepsi introduce a new version of their sodas and closely monitor them regarding how well they sell and what people think, you need to make a concerted effort to monitor your efforts.

You'll want to know:

- What students thought of the course? Was it challenging? Did it meet their expectations?
- What students and instructors thought of your technology? Easy to use? Confusing?
- Where did students find out about you? This will help you direct your marketing efforts.
- Was registration simple?
- If they contacted customer service, did they receive assistance? Was the process a smooth one?

Questionnaires, on-site surveys, and forms asking about instructors are all means of gathering feedback. Also, meeting or having regular discussions with instructors and technical staffers can keep you abreast of what needs to be addressed.

Feedback is often overlooked by many entrepreneurs until it is too late. Keep your eyes and ears open and be flexible enough to learn from what others are telling you. Good entrepreneurs know when their customers are telling them something and they respond accordingly.

Don't Forget the Check

Unlike many older educational institutions, you won't get funding from the government. And no one will float a bond issue if you run short of cash. You may be a natural-born business leader, teacher, or content creator, but you also have to close the sale. Whatever else you are doing and whatever your previous work history, you are the number-one salesperson for your own business.

So, how do you do that? Often, you must be creative just to get your foot in the door, but once in, you have to know in what direction to take your creativity. Forget the canned sales pitch. Listen to your customers, find what they need, and deliver creative ways of satisfying those needs.

Selling at all levels, whether selling your business model to a prospective investor or your courses to a corporation, means knowing your product inside and out. However, it does not mean that you cannot bend slightly to accommodate your buyers. There are always points that cannot deviate from the original plan. However, there are also times and places when a little flexibility goes a long way.

Morten Sohlberg of Sessions.edu reminds us that the traditional brick-and-mortar model of academia simply doesn't apply to online education. "Although we are a real educational company, we also very much have a bottom line," he notes. "We're a real company here to create an extraordinary user experience. But we need to make money. It's as simple as that. The way we operate our business will be very similar to any other business."

That means not forgetting to ask for the check. And keep asking when needed. You also want checks coming at you from more than one direction. As in any entrepreneurial venture, you want multiple revenue streams because many markets go through both boom times and bad times, sometimes because of seasonal fluctuations and other times because of the economy or poor management. How many classes, for instance, could you schedule for the week between Christmas and New Year's?

Examples of alternate revenue streams might be selling courseware as well as teaching courses, selling books that go along with courseware through your web site, and arranging affiliate relationships with other web sites to sell your goods. However, you also need some variety if you are working with corporate clients. Don't put all of your eggs in one basket unless you have a guaranteed contract and so much business from your one major client that you have no time to do work elsewhere. Otherwise, look for several clients so that when business slows on one end, you can boost it on another end.

Tip...

Smart Tip

Need to cast a nationwide marketing net for your IT certification training school? You can advertise or pay to get premium position in the search engines of IT web portals like Find Computer Schools (www.findcomputerschools.com). This has a powerful database of IT certification training resources searchable by training type, topic, certification type, state, zip code, and numerous other parameters. This is also true of other types of schools—there are portals out there on which you can be linked and web sites providing leads to schools just like yours focusing on a number of learning topics. Get yourself onto as many sites as possible through links and/or directory listings. Make sure, first, that the other site is legitimate and is doing some type of marketing. Being listed on a site that nobody knows about is a waste of time, and possibly money.

Once you enter a market, there typically are many subtle opportunities, some of which may even trump your original business model. Take Precision Information, for instance. It mass-markets CDs of its *Encyclopedia of Personal Finance*. It also sells these discs to wholesale buyers who then use them to educate different customer groups. Additionally, Precision will customize a portion of the content for financial service firms such as Ameritrade, Morningstar, and New York Life that focus on just a portion of the subject matter. And it licenses blocks of its content to consultants providing financial education to other groups.

"It's important for any company to have multiple revenue streams, and we planned it as well as we could from the start," says Precision chief executive Joe Saari. "But you never fully understand how they will evolve. You can never tell which will grow fastest or which revenue stream will turn out to be the richest vein. But they all leverage one another, and we know that we definitely want complementary revenue streams."

Keep your eyes and ears open, because some revenue streams will find you. For example, your foreign language students may be requesting dictionaries in CD or even book form; you can sell these, too, rather than referring them someplace else to purchase the dictionary they want.

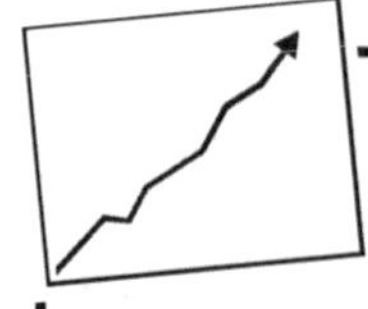

Stat Fact

One sales point is straightforward: Sixty-seven percent of respondents to a training survey cited cost savings as the most important benefit they derive from online training, according to Forrester Research.

What's an Entrepreneur?

Are you a teacher, a programmer, a computer geek, or an entrepreneur? Whatever it is that motivated you to embark on an online learning venture, you probably lack the full range of skills needed for success. You simply want to try to leverage your skills and find colleagues who will fill in the gaps.

Relevant experience is always good, but there is no particular educational or employment background that qualifies or disqualifies you from participating in the online education market. There is, as yet, no mandatory online education certification or specific training school for such a business. More important than experience is that indefinable quality of entrepreneurship. You make the leap. You put in the hours. You make the tough decisions.

Entrepreneurs like you cut across every socioeconomic and racial classification in the United States and the world. You can't be pinned down like butterflies on velvet. By definition, you are surprising and counterintuitive. You see opportunity where most of us see problems. You persevere when logic counsels retreat. You are a creator, and you are probably born to that role. You will get reshaped and tempered by the ventures in which you get involved. You'll need that flexibility in online learning as much as any other venture.

As an entrepreneur you are also bucking the odds. You have a dream itching to be fulfilled, so much so that you can't be content with a safe job. You have fire in the belly and are somewhat of a natural risk-taker.

Each entrepreneur takes a different path. There is no one right way to start a company, no step-by-step process, not even similar starting points for most entrepreneurs. Instead, it's all about recognizing opportunities, figuring out solutions, and working through the hurdles to realize your goal.

Whatever avenue of entrepreneurship you choose, be sure that you're doing something day in and day out that gives you pleasure and the kind of psychic rewards we all seek. Then at least, succeed or fail, it will have been a profitable experience. As Joe Saari of Precision Information puts it: "Do something you love, and you'll never work another day in your life."

Appendix
Online Education Business Resources

You've heard this saying: "Everything I know I learned in kindergarten." Yes, it was written by someone who grew up before the internet. In a little over a decade, the internet has become the vast resource for an amazing amount of information. It is the newspaper, magazine, and database resource of record for modern information.

While seeking information about online education, you will find a tremendous number of sites to browse, featuring more information than any single mind could possibly absorb.

If we were to publish only the names and addresses of education-related web sites, it would probably take a publication the size of the one you have just finished reading.

We'll leave it to you to lasso those areas of most interest to you. But here are some online web resources, as well as some offline contacts and recourses, to help you start your online education business.

Accreditation

Middle States Association of Colleges and Schools for Delaware, District of Columbia, Maryland, New Jersey, New York, Pennsylvania, Puerto Rico, Virgin Islands, www.msache.org.

New England Association of Schools and Colleges for Connecticut, Maine, Massachusetts, New Hampshire, Rhode Island, Vermont, www.neasc.org.

North Central Association of Colleges and Schools for Arizona, Arkansas, Colorado, Illinois, Indiana, Iowa, Kansas, Michigan, Minnesota, Missouri, Nebraska, New Mexico, North Dakota, Ohio, Oklahoma, South Dakota, West Virginia, Wisconsin, Wyoming, www.ncacihe.org.

The Northwest Commission on Colleges and Universities for Alaska, Idaho, Montana, Nevada, Oregon, Utah, Washington, www.cocnasc.org.

Southern Association of Colleges and Schools for Alabama, Florida, Georgia, Kentucky, Louisiana, Mississippi, North Carolina, South Carolina, Tennessee, Texas, Virginia, www.nwccu.org.

Western Association of Schools and Colleges for American Somoa, California, Hawaii, Guam, Trust Territory of the Pacific, www.wascweb.org.

Analysts and Experts

AberdeenGroup conducts an IT market analysis that measures the buying intentions of IT executives for application software categories and several technology infrastructure sectors, www.aberdeen.com.

comScore Networks researches consumer behavior on the internet, www.comscore.com.

Delphi Group custom research and strategic consulting in emerging technologies, www.delphigroup.com.

Employee Benefits Research Institute a nonprofit, nonpartisan research organization to advance public knowledge of the importance of employee benefits to the economy, www.ebri.org.

Ewing Marion Kauffman Foundation conducts research that defines what it takes to be a successful entrepreneur, studies best practices for supporting entrepreneurship and its role in the country's economy, and supports organizations and institutions that help entrepreneurs, www.emkf.org.

Forrester Research identifies and analyzes emerging trends in technology and their impact on business, www.forrester.com.

Gartner Viewpoint educational arm of broad-based qualitative and quantitative data researcher, www.gartner.com.

Goodmind market research firm using online research for competitive advantage, www.goodmind.net.

IDC Learning Services worldwide researcher of education markets, www.idc.com.

InsightExpress online market research of technology markets, www.insightexpress.com.

Market Data Retrieval provides mailing lists, database marketing services, state-by-state school directories, and statistical reports and analysis about the education market, www.schooldata.com.

Masie Center a learning lab, think tank, and learning consortium featuring 247 organizaitons including many major corpoations. www.masieweb.com.

Nielsen/NetRatings conducts an internet audience measurement service, tracking the entire spectrum of internet user behavior in more than 20 countries worldwide, representing nearly 90 percent of the global audience universe, www.nielsen-net ratings.com.

SCORE. Providing free expert counseling to new entrepreneurs by mostly retired experienced professionals and business executives, www.score.org.

Certification

CompTIA a global, 13,000-member IT trade group developing certification standards and best practices, www.comptia.org.

Institute for Certification of Computer Professionals nonprofit group dedicated to the establishment of professional standards in the computer industry, www.iccp.org.

International Association for Continuing Education and Training nonprofit association certifying providers of continuing education and training programs, www.iacet.org.

International Information Systems Security Certification Consortium a nonprofit organization providing security practices training and certification to information security professionals worldwide, having certified over 42,000 information security professionals in more than 110 countries, www.isc2.org.

The Council for Higher Education Accreditation (CHEA) answers frequently-asked questions about accreditation and many resources; CHEA represents more than 3,000 colleges and universities, www.chea.org.

Government Agencies

Bureau of Labor Statistics. Part of the Department of Labor, measures nationwide labor and occupational trends, www.bls.gov.

Census Bureau. A good source of demographic information, www.census.gov.

Department of Education. Cabinet-level department devoted to educational issues and research, www.ed.gov.

Internal Revenue Service. Providing the tax information and forms that you will need, www.irs.gov.

National Center for Education Statistics. The primary U.S. federal agency for collecting and analyzing data on education worldwide; provides an extensive list of statistical tables, charts, and studies reporting on the condition and progress of education, nces.ed.gov.

National Education Association (NEA). The nation's largest employee organization, NEA has over 3.2 million members in all levels of education, www.nea.org.

Small Business Administration. A source of possible funding and plenty of useful information for the small-business person, www.sba.gov.

Social Security Administration. Projections on demographics, www.ssa.gov.

United States Patent and Trademark Office (USPTO). The government source for obtaining trademarks or patents and information on both accounts, www.uspto.gov.

Magazines and Newsletters

Certification Magazine. A monthly magazine covering the certification market, www.certmag.com.

Chronicle of Higher Education. Weekly news source for college and university faculty members and administrators, www.chronicle.com.

eLearn Magazine. Published by ACM, a not-for-profit educational association serving workers who teach and learn in computing-related fields, www.elearn.org

e-learning Magazine. A monthly magazine covering e-learning and especially corporate training, www.elearning.b2bmediaco.com.

eSchool News. A monthly newspaper to help K through12 decision makers use technology and the internet to achieve educational goals, www.eschoolnews.com.

ITWorld. A collection of newsletters, white papers, IT news, and web cast sites published by Accela Communications, whose parent company is IDG, www.itworld.com.

Technology & Learning Magazine. A publication for early adopters of technology in education, www.techlearning.com.

The Complete K-12 Newsletter. Produced by Education Market Research, specializing in K through 12 school/library market research, www.ed-market.com.

T.H.E. Journal magazine and newsletters offered by T.H.E., an association for educators, www.thejournal.com.

Training magazine. A professional development magazine that advocates training and work force development as a business tool, www.trainingmag.com.

Workindex.com. Newsletter produced by the publishers of Human Resource Executive in cooperation with Cornell University's School of Industrial Labor Relations; links to more than 4,000 workplace-related web sites; offers HR news and tools, www.workindex.com.

Books

Fusions: Integrating Values in Online Education by Jane M. Govoni, Mary M. Govoni, Mary T. Spoto, and Valerie Wright Kendall, Hunt Publishing, (2006).

Interactive Online Education: Implications for Theory and Practice (The Open and Flexible Learning Series) by Charles Juwah, Routledge, (2006).

Online Education: Global Questions, Local Answers (Technical Communications Series) by Kelli Cargile Cook and Keith Grant-Davie, Baywood Publishing Company, (2005).

Online Education Learning and Teaching in Cyberspace by Greg Kearsley, Wadsworth/Thomson Custom Publishing, (2004).

Peterson's Guide to Online Learning by Fern A. Oram, Peterson's Guides, (2005).

Software and Services

Adobe online learning products, case studies, white papers, delivery and management systems, and more, including Adobe Reader, www.adobe.com.

Blackboard e-learning software and services, www.blackboard.com.

Business Plan Write business plan software from Business Resource Software, www.brs-inc.com.

Microsoft Media Player, Windows video, audio player, and other platforms and services for online learning are all available from Microsoft, www.microsoft.com.

RealOne Player video and audio player from RealNetworks, www.realnetworks.com.

Resolution from Ncompass Labs, workflow-based document creation tool. This company has recently been acquired by Microsoft, so you will be led to their web site, www.ncompass.com.

Saba Learning. An internet-based learning management system from Saba Systems, a developer of human capital development and management solutions, also includes software from Centra, with whom it merged, www.saba.com.

WebEx carrier-class communication services enabling users to share presentations, documents, applications, voice, and video spontaneously in a seamless environment, www.webex.com.

Successful Online Education Entrepreneurs

Brainbench, www.brainbench.com

Capella University, www.capellauniversity.edu

CourseBridge, www.coursebridge.com

Devry University, www.devry.edu/online_options.jsp

eLearners, www.elearners.com

Jones International University, www.jonesinternational.edu

Kaplan University, www.getinfo.kaplan.edu/Microsite_B/index.aspx

Learners Online, www.learnersonline.com

LearnKey, www.learnkey.com

MiraCosta College, www.miracosta.edu/Instruction/DistanceEducation/index.cfm

Phoenix University, www.phoenix.edu

Sessions School of Design, www.sessions.edu

Sprylearning Co., www.sprylearning.com

Walden University, www.waldenu.edu

Western Governors University, www.wgu.edu

Westwood College, www.westwoodonline.edu

Trade Groups, Associations, and Organizations

American Association of Community Colleges (AACA) nationwide trade group for community colleges, www.aacc.nche.edu.

American Association of Retired Persons (AARP) a nonprofit membership organization for people 50 and over, providing information and resources, legislative advocacy, and other member services; publisher of *Modern Maturity* and *My Generation* magazines, www.aarp.org.

American Association of School Administrators (AASA) a professional organization for more than 14,000 elementary and secondary educational leaders across the United States and overseas, www.aasa.org.

American Council on Education (ACE) international membership organization devoted to adult and higher education issues, www.acenet.edu.

American Distance Education Consortium (ADEC) an international consortium of educators devoted to distance learning, www.adec.edu.

American School Directory (ASD) an omnibus internet site with information on K-12 schools nationwide, www.asd.com.

American Society of Training and Development (ASTD) U.S. chapter of a worldwide trade association for workplace learning, forming a world-class community of practice for 70,000 members in more than 100 countries, www.astd.org.

Association for Computing Machinery (ANM) worldwide association of 75,000 members devoted to computing; a $99 annual subscription provides access to more than a million pages of IT-related content and 200 online training courses on the ACM portal, www.acm.org.

eLearning Guild a membership community for online learning professionals, featuring resources, networking opportunities, and publications, www.elearningguild.com.

K–12 School Networking Conference annual networking event for K–12 educators featuring speakers, workshops, and a tradeshow, www.k12schoolnetworking.org.

The National Association of Graduate-Professional Students (NAGPS) is a nonprofit organization dedicated to improving the quality of graduate and professional student life in the United States, www.nagps.org.

National Venture Capital Association (NVCA) trade association representing the venture capital industry with a membership of 400-plus VC firms and organizations that manage pools of risk equity capital, www.nvca.org.

RTPnet a nonprofit organization promoting electronic communication, www.rtp net.org/comp.

Society for Human Resource Management (SHRM) association of human resource professionals, www.shrm.org.

Society for Technical Communications (STC) an 18,000-member organization, in eight regions (20 local chapters) including technical writers, editors, graphic designers, multimedia artists, web and intranet page information designers, and others whose work involves technical communications, www.stc.org.

United States Distance Learning Association (USDLA) a consortium of organizations devoted to the expansion of distance learning, www.usdla.org.

World Association for Online Education a nonprofit organization developed to support and evaluate online education based on the voluntary efforts of educators, worldwide, www.waoe.org.

Web Sites

Bisk University Alliance consortium of e-learning colleges and universities, www.bisk.com.

Bplan.com all about writing business plans, with examples, plus you can buy the latest version of Business Plan Pro software from Palo Alto.

CareerExchange.com extensive job search database with online conferencing and a people-match program, www.careerexchange.com.

ClassesUSA a web portal, featuring courses from online and traditional universities, which can be selected by subject or university, www.classesusa.com.

Continue2learn.net more than 500 self-paced, real-time interactive training courses over the internet, www.continue2learn.net.

EducationToGo college-oriented e-learning portal, www.ed2go.com.

Educator's Reference Desk information from and links to a tremendous number of resources, www.eduref.org.

e-Learning Center gives ideas, tips, and solutions on how to sharpen your skills and increase your knowledge, regardless of profession, www.e-learningcenter.com.

eLearningDepot a catalog of more than 1,000 courses offering e-learning programs and certification training for businesses and individuals, http://elearningdepot.com.

eLearning Technology site featuring information about online learning plus numerous blogs, www.elearningtech.blogspot.com.

Find Computer Schools an IT web portal with a powerful database of IT certification training searchable by training type, topic, certification type, state, zip code, and other parameters, www.find-computer-schools.com.

Guidetoonlineschools.com large portal for accedited colleges, universities, and distance-learning programs.

Homeschool.com a comprehensive site featuring all sorts of information and links to everything related to schooling children at home.

Hostway provider of web hosting services and online business tools for small to medium-sized enterprises, supporting more than 100,000 web sites worldwide, www.hostway.com.

HR.com information, resources, products, and services for individuals in human resource management, www.hr.com.

NicheBoards.com an alliance of several leading niche employment web sites to help narrow your search for instructors and other workers, www.nicheboards.com.

Oracle University web portal with training, certification information, and other resources for the broad set of computer tools produced by Oracle, www.oracle.com.

Selling to Schools an online magazine for educational technology professionals, www.sellingtoschools.com.

TechTutorials.net a directory of almost 2,000 free computer tutorials and white papers, www.techtutorials.net.

The Trade Show Coach includes articles, books, tapes, workshops, and free weekly e-mail tips to help you get the most out of your trade show experience, www.TheTradeShow Coach.com.

WorkSpace Resources online source for information about the working environment, ergonomics, design, and the contract furniture industry, www.workspace-resources.com.

World Wide Learn web portal providing an independent directory of educational services and resources as well as hundreds of online courses in numerous subject categories, www.WorldWideLearn.com.

Glossary

Accreditation. Being granted approval to give educational credits by having a knowledge base that formally meets the standards and requirements of a university, government, trade, or other recognized accrediting body.

Asynchronous learning. Learning through the use of asynchronous communication, whereby there is a delay in the interaction. Self-paced courses, courses on CD-ROM, as well as those via e-mail or even on message boards all fall into this category because there is a time gap until the respondent communicates a message back. Students can, therefore, maintain their own pace.

Audit. To audit a course means to participate without receiving credit, or in some cases, without paying the full fee. In the latter case, students are typically only allowed to audit a few classes before being asked to pay for the course.

Blended learning. A course that utilizes more than one form of learning, typically including in-person classroom work and online course materials.

Certification. Acknowledgement that a student has successfully completed a course of study—usually measured by passing an exam—that prepares him or her to work in a specific field or with a specific technology.

CGI scripts. Small programs that transfer a web page visitor to another page when a hyperlink is selected.

Chat. A situation whereby two or more people are typing messages in an online room or forum. Chats are often used for discussions of coursework with other students or with the instructor.

Computer-Based Training (CBT). A fully automated learning environment in which there is no actual instructor; all work is preprogrammed and designed so that the student interacts with the computer for assignments, tests or quizzes, questions and answers, etc. This system requires advanced technology training to set up and maintain.

Concentration. A specific area of study, such as business or marketing, in which the student takes a set of courses, typically for a degree in a particular area.

Course Management System (CMS). A software environment for developing, delivering, and administering courses; also see Learning Management System.

CPM—Cost-per-thousand impressions. The minimum number of ad views against which advertising rates are applied.

Demographic category. A characteristic or classification of a group, used primarily for marketing purposes, for example, gender or a specific age range (18 to 29).

Distance education. From the old correspondence courses (by snail mail) to the modern online educational courses that you will be offering, any learning by which the two parties (student and teacher) are not in the same location is considered distance learning. Face to face learning (F2F), with the student and educator in the same place, is the opposite.

Domain. A collection of web pages associated with a unique domain name registered with one of the authorized registrars, for example, Yahoo.com

HTML—Hypertext Markup Language. The coding language widely used to present web pages.

Java. A compact but powerful scripting language originally launched by Sun Microsystems for creating small applets for the internet; now very widely used.

Learning Management System (LMS). A full-service software environment that contains an extensive set of learning tools, which may include synchronous and/or asynchronous course presentation, various conferencing options, data storage and bulletin board services for students, administration tools, and many other services.

Multiple revenue streams. Having revenue from more than one activity or class of customers; an example would be selling online courses to corporations as well as CD-ROMs to educational institutions.

Streaming media. Multimedia sent over the internet in a "stream" rather than in a single file.

Syllabus. The overview of the course as planned by the instructor, typically within the parameters of the school and/or state requirements. The syllabus includes the course goals and objectives as well as the books that will be used, reports and other assignments, and tests to be given.

Synchronous learning. A means whereby learning takes place with both parties participating at the same time without a delay in the communication, such as streaming video.

Threaded discussion. Messages posted that are on the same topic, often used in online education. The common theme threads the messages together. This is one means by which students can interact with each other as well as with the instructor.

Top level domain. A group of internet domains that end with a common suffix—such as .com, .net, or .edu—managed by a single domain registrar under the authority of the Internet Corporation for Assigned Names and Numbers (ICANN).

Unique audience. Internet advertising metric measuring the number of individuals that have gone to a site at least once during the defined time period.

Vendor-neutral certification. IT certification examining a student's knowledge of generalized technology, such as local-area networking, rather than the technology from a specific vendor such as Microsoft.

Vendor-specific certification. IT certification examining a student's qualifications to work with a specific vendor's technology.

Virtual classroom. An online classroom in cyberspace that doesn't actually exist in the real world. This is the usual online learning environment.

Virtual private network. Technology that creates a private, secure tunnel through the public internet; it can connect multiple sites or individuals and allow them to communicate, collaborate, and share files securely.

Whiteboard. An internet variation on a longtime computer technology and a part of many LMSs, it provides for content displayed on one PC to be simultaneously displayed on other internet-connected PCs.

XML—Extensible Mark-up Language. A data description standard that is the successor to HTML. It is much more programmable and permits greater interaction with databases.

Index